W9-DEU-377

"Doug Bentley has drawn on his extensive knowledge of the scriptures and his many years of experience as an exemplary Seminary teacher to provide a resource intended to be an aid for conversion of investigators of the Church of Jesus Christ of Latter-day Saints.

"The background given in his discussion of birthright, covenant and other biblical and religious doctrines, uses scripture to entice the unbeliever to accept the challenge of believing. Judicious use of his work by the reader could awaken, in an investigator, a challenge to pray and seek the spirit to help lead to his acceptance and conversion."

—*Maurice D. Watts, mission president,*
Australia, Sidney Mission 1982-1985

"*Abraham's Seed and Covenant* is an excellent work in giving the chronological, sequential and logical structure of the truth our Heavenly Father and His son Jesus Christ have revealed for all of us here on earth. Approaching the revealed truth from this perspective should make it much easier for those who are familiar with teachings of Christ to come to a knowledge of who He is and who they are in the eyes of God. All mankind's true, eternal heritage comes to life in this work."

—*David R. Broadhead, mission president,*
Japan, Nagoya Mission, 1985-1988,
and of the Japan Missionary Training Center, 2000-2002

"If you truly want to have a testimony, and know why you should have it, then Doug Bentley's book is a must read. He puts it in black and white, who we are and our responsibilities. For we who might be nervous about missionary work, there is no excuse now. Not only do we have the answers but we can now give Brother Bentley's book to those who are searching for their own pilgrimage of truth, and they will find it."

—*Dr. Scott F. Smith, Ph.D.*

ABRAHAM'S
SEED
AND COVENANT

ABRAHAM'S SEED
AND COVENANT

BY DOUGLAS T. BENTLEY

Springville, Utah

Copyright © 2003 Douglas T. Bentley

All Rights Reserved.

No part of this book may be reproduced in any form whatsoever, whether by graphic, visual, electronic, film, microfilm, tape recording, or any other means, without prior written permission of the author, except in the case of brief passages embodied in critical reviews and articles.

ISBN: 1-55517-706-9
e. 2

Published by Cedar Fort, Inc.
www.cedarfort.com

Distributed by:

Cover design by Nicole Cunningham
Cover design © 2003 by Lyle Mortimer

Printed in the United States of America
10 9 8 7 6 5 4 3 2 1

Printed on acid-free paper

Library of Congress Control Number: 2003110343

To my parents,
who worked so hard to raise me on the right path,
who taught me the Gospel of Jesus Christ,
supported me in my missionary endeavors,
and who have been an undying example and blessing
of service to all that have known them.

And to my wife and children,
who are the joy, fulfillment, and love of my life.

CONTENTS

INTRODUCTION

Throughout the annals of time, different religious factions have debated long and hard over the truth and veracity of their particular organizations, as well as their interpretation of differing Christian doctrine. People have even been put to death in the name of Christianity. With all of the differing on religious mores, and points of doctrine, how can a person come to a rational conclusion regarding which denomination to align themselves with?

The vast majority of modern religion has one major focal point from which they all evolved . . . Father Abraham. The Jewish Nation has long prided itself in the fact that they are the direct descendants of this great ancient Prophet/Patriarch, and in fact, this focal point extends to the nation of Islam as well. The Islamic prophet Muhammad himself proclaimed that the gospel he taught was nothing more than a restoration of the gospel of Abraham. Many individuals have struggled to try and find some sort of common ground between their chosen "church," and the teachings of the ancient prophets revealed in the Holy Bible . . . but to no avail. It seems that someone can always find a particular scripture that appears to contradict any given teaching. With such a universal starting point as Abraham, surely there must be a common story-line, or thread, if you will, that can be used by any sincere seeker of the truth to identify the correct path they are to take in that quest for the that truth. As a matter of fact there is such a thread . . . if one truly understands the entirety of the covenant that God the Father made with this ancient patriarch, Abraham. For it is the fulfillment of that covenant which is basically the storyline of the entire Bible, and will continue to unfold until Jesus Christ, the Savior of the world, comes again in His resurrected Glory.

This book examines that story, and presents the doctrinal facts, begun in the Old Testament . . . and continued into the

New Testament of the King James Version of the Bible. Frankly, and in a simple format . . . that story is this: The Lord designated the family of the ancient patriarch, Abraham, as "His Covenant Family." Abraham had come from an idolatrous family, but through his faith and obedience, overcame that deficit, and followed the path of the Holy Priesthood (patriarchal order), which had been established by God the Father- with Adam, and carried on through his lineage by the likes of Seth, Enoch, and Noah. By the time of Abraham, idol worship had become rampant among the children of Adam. But Abraham sought the blessings of the fathers through the obtaining of the holy priesthood of God. He paid tithes and offerings to the great high priest Melchizedek (of whom the high priesthood was called because of his righteousness), and sought the direction of his God, under the direction of that priesthood.

The God of Heaven heard Abraham's supplications, and rewarded him richly for his dedication in seeking to live the ways of the fathers. He established a special covenant with this great patriarch, and with his seed after him. All of that seed, that were willing to enter into that same "Abrahamic Covenant" would be entitled to the blessings contained therein. Those blessings were: a numerous posterity, which would continue into the eternities, and the right to the holy priesthood with its inherent powers and keys. He was likewise promised that his seed would be given certain lands as an eternal inheritance, and that through the holy priesthood, which was bestowed upon them, they would be the means of bringing salvation and exaltation to the entire human race—as many as would hearken to the commandments of the Eternal Father, and be willing to enter into the covenant, as a token of the profession of their loyalty to Abraham's God.

Abraham and his wife Sarah were childless, but were promised in the covenant that they would be blessed with a bounteous posterity. Abraham was given plural wives—the first being Sarah, the wife of the covenant. He had posterity through Hagar, Sarah's handmaid (Ishmael) through whom descended the Arab Nations- and the religion of Islam. He also married a woman named Keturah in his old age, and through her loins had a multitude of descendants as well. However, it was through Sarah, his chosen, covenant wife—that the blessings of the priesthood would be perpetuated, and through whom the Abrahamic Covenant would be fulfilled. It was to be through this lineage that all of the families of the earth would be blessed.

A sound understanding of this sacred pact between God, and a man, is absolutely requisite if a person is going to be able to make sense of the Bible . . . and its subsequent story. This book explains that covenant, and the accompanying story so simply yet so clearly, that the reader will be able to see the grand plan of the Eternal Father for His spirit sons and daughters, here in mortality.

To Abraham and Sarah was born a son named Isaac, to whom the rights of the priesthood, and the covenant were perpetuated. Isaac, in turn, had twin sons- Esau and Jacob. Esau, though he was the eldest, showed no regard for the righteousness required of the birthright son, according to the covenant. As a result, the covenant blessing was passed on to Jacob, whom the scriptures tell us, was upright and sober toward the things of God . . . and of the fathers. The God of Heaven appeared to Jacob, and changed his named to Israel (One who prevails with God), in conjunction with the re-establishment of the Abrahamic Covenant, with Jacob. From this event, forth... the God of the children of Abraham is referred to in scripture as the God of Abraham, Isaac, and Jacob. The name Israel also refers to the descendants of Israel, as well as their kingdom, and is used to denote (1) Jacob (2) his literal descendants. And (3) true believers of Christ, regardless of their lineage or geographical location.

According to the account in the book of Genesis, Israel had twelve sons, from four different wives. There was a major power struggle when Israel, in much the same manner that his father had done with him, gave the birthright to Joseph—who was not the eldest of his sons. This resulted again, because as it was with

Esau, the elder brothers didn't measure up spiritually to the standard set by the Lord for the Patriarch of this chosen, covenant line. Joseph married and had two sons, Manasseh, and Ephraim, to whom he bestowed the blessings of the birthright.

The children of Israel lived in Egypt for roughly 430 years, until they were led out of bondage by Moses, and into the promised land of Canaan, by Joshua, who himself was a member of the tribe of Ephraim. Shortly after entering the Promised Land, there was a great deal of enmity between the tribes of Ephraim, and Judah. These bad feelings resulted in a rift, and subsequent separation of the tribes into separate kingdoms. The Northern Kingdom consisted of ten of the tribes, and was led by the tribe of Ephraim. They were known in the scriptures as Israel. The Southern Kingdom consisted of the tribe of Judah, and part of the tribe of Benjamin. It was known as Judah, and was ruled by that tribe.

Idolatry led to apostasy on the parts of both kingdoms, and eventually the Northern Kingdom was conquered by the Assyrian Empire, and carried away captive to the north countries. Thus they became known as the "Lost Ten Tribes." Approximately 135 years after the downfall of the Northern Kingdom, the Kingdom of Judah followed suit. This time it was at the hands of King Nebuchadnezzar, and the Babylonian Empire. There were different conquests made which resulted in changes in power between that time and the time of the birth of Jesus Christ. As a result of all of this, the birthright tribe of Ephraim became a lost tribe. So how could the promise in the covenant made with Abraham be fulfilled concerning his seed blessing all of the nations and families of the earth?

There are many prophecies recorded in the Old Testament concerning the fulfillment of this promise, but suffice it to say that the one of most importance, is that in the last days, prior to the Second Coming of the Messiah, a remnant of the birthright tribe of Ephraim, will be raised up to gather the scattered members of the blood of Israel. The prophet Ezekiel, one of the last prophets to witness against the Kingdom of Judah, before their fall, prophesied that this remnant of Ephraim would need to have a second record, in addition to the record of Judah (The Bible) in order to commence this prophetic gathering. That record he said was the record of the house of Joseph, the birthright tribe. All of Christianity knows about the record of Judah (Bible), but where is the missing stick or record of the birthright tribe of Joseph? His was the right to preside over the tribes of Israel, and to bring the world unto salvation.

Where on the earth is a people who claim to be descendants of that birthright tribe? And who claim to have the missing record of Joseph, which must be used along with the Bible, by that tribe, in gathering the scattered remnants of the house of Israel? What of them? How important would it be to know of such happenings, if one really wanted to be assured of the correct affiliation with the authority necessary to effect their salvation?

That is sole purpose of this book! The remnant of Ephraim has risen up, and the prophesied Book of Joseph is in his hand. He is going forth as "A stone cut out of the mountain without hands," to quote the prophet Daniel, (who was part of that conquest by Babylon) Israel is being gathered, and the majority of the world knows nothing of the prophecy—or of its imminent fulfillment. That stone will continue to roll forth until it fills the whole earth.

It is the responsibility, and the duty of Ephraim, to carry out this great work. The work of God will be accomplished, and no unhallowed hand can stop its progress. This book lays out the Father's plan for that great gathering. The doctrine is irrefutable—it is the story of the Bible. Being a descendant of Abraham, in and of itself, is not enough to guarantee anyone anything. John The Baptist illustrated this fact when he was dealing with the ancient Jewish leaders, who took comfort in the fact that they had descended from Abraham. In Matthew 3:7-12 we read:

> 7 But when he saw many of the Pharisees and Sadducees come to his baptism, he said unto them, O generation of vipers, who hath warned you to flee from the wrath to come?

8   Bring forth therefore fruits meet for repentance:

9   And think not to say within yourselves, We have Abraham to our father: for I say unto you, that God is able of these stones to raise up children unto Abraham.

10 And now also the axe is laid unto the root of the trees: therefore every tree which bringeth not forth good fruit is hewn down, and cast into the fire.

11 I indeed baptize you with water unto repentance: but he that cometh after me is mightier than I, whose shoes I am not worthy to bear: he shall baptize you with the Holy Ghost, and with fire:

12 Whose fan is in his hand, and he will thoroughly purge his floor, and gather his wheat into the garner; but he will burn up the chaff with unquenchable fire (Matthew 3:7-12.)

We must be joined with the covenants made with Abraham, and then honor those covenants . . . if we would feign to lay claim to the blessings of Abraham. Those covenants are only to be obtained from the hand of the house of Joseph, who alone holds the birthright. So where are those authorized servants?

The real questions we must each ask ourselves are: do we know, and believe, the prophecies of the Bible? And if what is contained in this book reveals the fulfillment of those sacred Prophecies, what would we be giving up if we failed to acknowledge, and secure, the wealth of sacred information that comprises the missing "Stick of Joseph." If that record is what it proclaims to be, the obtaining of the blessings of the covenant of Abraham lie with the Church that brought it forth. The End is nigh at hand, yea even at the doors. If we fail to know all there is to know concerning what is required of us, will we be ready for that day? It is only when we are not afraid of the truth that we will truly find it. May the Spirit of the Lord witness the truth to you, in your search for these answers as you read the pages of *Abraham's Seed and Covenant.*

FOREWORD

As a convert to the Church of Jesus Christ of Latter-day Saints at the age of 50 years, I can say without hesitation that I would have been light years ahead in my understanding of the restored gospel of Jesus Christ as recorded in the Book of Mormon, if I had first had the opportunity to read *Abraham's Seed and Covenant* before I had met with the LDS missionaries. Being a practicing Methodist all of my life before joining the Church, I had certain Christian beliefs that made it more difficult to understand and accept the teaching of the Church. I, like others that are of different faiths; have had the misconception that the Book of Mormon was a replacement book of scripture for the Holy Bible. However, in the years since my conversion through study and prayer, I've come to understand that it is a companion book to the Holy Bible and contains, like the Bible, a volume of holy scripture which is a record of God's dealing with the ancient inhabitants of the Americas and contains, as does the Bible, the fullness of the everlasting gospel. But until I was introduced to the book *Abraham's Seed and Covenant* as a study guide, one that refers back in many instances directly to scriptural passages from the Holy Bible, I had difficulty understanding the connection between the two books.

Speaking as a convert to the Church, I highly recommend to anyone who is seriously investigating the Church of Jesus Christ of Latter-day Saints, that they obtain a copy of this invaluable tool that will make clear the undeniable connection between these two books of holy record. It has been inspirational reading and has answered countless questions that I have had difficulty in resolving to my satisfaction.

Herbert C. Davis

For there are many yet on the earth among all sects, parties, and denominations, who are blinded by the subtle craftiness of men, whereby they lie in wait to deceive, and who are only kept from the truth because they know not where to find it—

Therefore, that we should waste and wear out our lives in bringing to light all the hidden things of darkness, wherein we know them; and they are truly manifest from heaven—

These should then be attended to with great earnestness.

Doctrine and Covenants 123:12-14

1. *Now the Lord had said unto Abram, Get thee out of thy country, and from thy kindred, and from thy father's house, unto a land that I will shew thee:*
2. *And I will make of thee a great nation, and I will bless thee, and make thy name great; and thou shalt be a blessing:*
3. *And I will bless them that bless thee, and curse them that curseth thee: and in thee shall all families of the earth be blessed.*

—Genesis 12:1-3

CHAPTER 1
A COVENANT IS CUT

Modern Christianity today can present some perplexing problems for many would-be followers. With hundreds and perhaps thousands of different denominations dotting the land, how is a person supposed to know which one to join himself/herself with? Will every road eventually lead one back to "heaven," or is there just one "true" church? If the former is true it doesn't matter which church we choose to join. If it be the latter, then it makes all the difference in the world whom we choose to affiliate ourselves with. In fact, it may be the single most important decision that we will ever make in this life.

Somebody once said: "Who we are now will determine what we are hereafter." If that is the case we had better be anxiously engaged in being the best that we can possibly be right now. And we had best be careful to affiliate ourselves with that which will have the power to enable us to return one day again into our Heavenly Father's presence. In his letter to the Ephesians, the Apostle Paul informs us that there is "One Lord, one faith, and one baptism" (Ephesians 4:5). If that is the case, can just anyone perform that ordinance for us, or does that person need some special qualification to perform it?

1

In John 3:5 the Savior informed us that unless we are baptized we cannot receive of His kingdom. Does it really make a difference whether it is done by immersion, sprinkling, or simply a baptism of the heart by accepting Jesus, or in some other alternative manner?

Many and varying are religionist's viewpoints on this topic. As important as these requirements are to our salvation, surely the answers are clearly explained in the Bible, aren't they? No, as a matter of fact, they aren't. Things are so vague on many points of doctrine that a person can find scriptures that seem to support just about any point of view that they may come up with. Perhaps that's why Paul also said that people in our day would be "ever learning, and never able to come to the knowledge of the truth" (2 Timothy 3:7).

Of major importance is the issue of authority. In Hebrews 5:4 we are told that authority isn't something that we can just assume ourselves, but rather must be bestowed upon us by one of the Lord's anointed servants, as was Aaron. The Savior was constantly rebuking the Sadducees and Pharisees for acting without the proper authority from him. So where do the majority of the worlds' religious leaders claim to have received their authority? Was it from God himself, or do they claim to have received it by going to some form of school, or through some type of program? Some of this countries "ordained ministers" have apparently even obtained their ministerial certificates through mail order, with no more training or legitimacy than to send their money in for it.

Will the Lord recognize ordinances performed by such an one as valid? Or will he say to them as he makes elusion to in Matthew, to depart from him those who worked iniquity? Those who assume to represent him without his authorization are surely among those he strongly reprimanded, saying their works were in vain, having been performed without his seal of approval or endorsement (see Matthew 7:21-23). To understand the importance of the authority he was referring to, an understanding of the Old Testament is vital.

Whenever the Father has desired to bless His children, He

has chosen to do it through the use of covenant making. Possibly the most widely known of those covenants is what is referred to as the Abrahamic Covenant. Now the Lord had said unto Abram,

Get thee out of thy country, and from thy kindred, and from thy father's house, unto a land that I will show thee.

And I will make of thee a great nation, and I will bless thee, and make thy name great; and thou shalt be a blessing:

And I will bless them that bless thee, and curse him that curseth thee: and in thee shall all families of the earth be blessed (Genesis 12:1-3).

Abraham was tested severely, being denied offspring until he was old, and then being asked to offer Isaac, the heir that he had so long waited for. The fact that Abraham would do as he was asked in sacrificing his only son would seem in itself to be hard enough, but from his own writings we learn of the depth of his conviction to serve God at all costs.

Abraham had been where Isaac was going to be, on a sacrificial altar as a young man, and I am sure would have had total empathy for the feelings and emotions that his treasured son would experience.

It must have been all that he could do to climb Mt. Moriah that gloomy day and prepare to make the ultimate sacrifice, the very same mountain that centuries later our Heavenly Father would offer his only begotten son on. But climb the mountain he did, and with a heavy heart, he proceeded to do as God commanded. Through this willingness to lay all, on the altar, Abraham showed his true convictions, and God rewarded him richly for it.

God established the covenant with Abraham that he had previously promised to bestow. Through this covenant special blessings and privileges were to be extended to him and his posterity (see Genesis 15:1-7, 22:15-18; 35:9-12). Included in those blessings would be the right to the priesthood, the power of God, given to man to act in his name and have it recognized by him as binding.

Another major part of the covenant was that he would be blessed with an endless posterity, as numerous as the stars in the heavens or the sands of the sea. And it would be through that posterity that God would choose to bless the entire earth with the blessings of that covenant.

Customary to the times was that the eldest or firstborn son would be designated as the birthright son (see Deuteronomy 21:15-17). This son would receive a double portion of the father's inheritance. This extra portion was to be used to take care of the parents in their old age and to help the rest of the family as needed. It would be his responsibility, because the second part designated the birthright son as the leader of the family once the father was gone.

Peculiar to the covenant was the fact that personal right- eousness played a greater part than particular birth order. In other words, if the eldest were unrighteous, the birthright would be taken from him and given to another (see Genesis 35:22; 49:3-4). Thus, age didn't necessarily guarantee the obtaining of the birthright. With Abraham, as was the case with many of the prophets of old, God gave them other wives and concubines. If the eldest son of the first wife proved unworthy, the birthright would then fall upon the shoulders of the eldest son of the second wife (see 1 Chronicles 5:1-2).

The birthright was of great importance, so much so, that as I will illustrate in chapter 2, people were willing to even kill a brother to obtain it. Such was the case with Jacob and Esau [Genesis 25:29-34, 27:41-45]. At any rate, the birthright carried with it two major things; first, financial gain, and second, honor or status as the patriarch of the family.

Abraham had a son born to him before Isaac came along. His name was Ishmael, but he was born to Hagar, Sarah's maid who was given to Abraham as a concubine (see Genesis 16:1-6; 21:9-21). Thus was the birthright given to Isaac, and not Ishmael who was many years his senior. To those not familiar with the covenant, this might seem like Ishmael was wronged, or even robbed. But to those who have made special covenants with God, and are diligent in keeping those covenants, it is understood that the correct son was chosen to carry on and perpetuate the covenant. Indeed, Abraham was truly a prophet, so he surely made the right selection. That decision has not been a popular one in the eyes of Ishmael's posterity (the Arab nations) over the millennia that have followed. Much of fighting has taken place, continuing today, over just who it was that was the rightful heir to the land considered sacred by them and by the inhabitants (Jews) of present day Palestine. In fact, it appears that this war will continue to rage on until the last battle to end all battles is staged in those very streets, and the Savior himself returns to settle the dispute at Armageddon.

The story of Isaac and Rebekah is a remarkable illustration to the importance of marrying within the covenant, and the extreme lengths that God, our Father, would have us go to ensure it. Perhaps there were no eligible women in Canaan of the covenant lineage who caught his fancy, or maybe the grass just seemed greener in other pastures. Esau thought so little of the covenant that he married twice to daughters of Canaan, outside the faith of his father. Jacob, on the other hand, was sent a great distance to the house of his mother's brother, Laban, to seek a wife in order to ensure that the covenant would continue through him (see Genesis 27:46; 28:1-5). True, he also did it to avoid the wrath of Esau, who had sold it to him earlier for a mess of pottage. But the Lord had designated years earlier that Jacob, not Esau was to have the birthright.

Jacob, in turn, had ten sons, by two wives and two concubines. Reuben the eldest son, born to Jacob and his first wife Leah, was first in line for the coveted assignment. But he made a major error of judgment when he committed adultery with Bilhah, the maid of Rachel, who had been given by God to Jacob as a concubine, and who also bore him two sons, Dan and Naphtali. Their offspring later became two of the lost ten tribes (see Genesis 35:16-26). Reuben's sin with his father's handmaid cost him his right to the birthright (see Genesis 49: 3-4; I Chronicles 5: 1-2). So with Reuben's fall from grace the birthright went to the eldest son of his second wife Rachel, who was the younger sister of Leah. That son born to Jacob in his old age was none other than Joseph who would later be sold into slavery for a few pieces of silver by his older brothers because of jealousy over the birthright. Joseph proved himself worthy of the blessings of the birthright by keeping his covenants, despite tremendous opposition during this trying ordeal.

Because of his integrity and faithfulness, Joseph rose from the dungeons of Egypt to the second in command to Pharaoh (see Genesis 39: 3-6; 41: 37-45). Because of his gift of interpreting the pharaoh's dream, Joseph was assigned to be in charge of Egypt's granaries, and he stockpiled a surplus of food for seven years. When Jacob (Israel) and his family ran out of food, they were forced to come to Egypt to buy grain. It was then that Joseph was able to preserve Jacob and his house from perishing with hunger (see Genesis 45: 9-28; 46: 1-7; 29-30). Israel was given the land of Goshen as a place to reside because of Joseph's influence in Egypt, and there they resided for some four hundred years. A good portion of those years, were spent as slaves, when Egypt was overthrown and the Hyksos people were replaced as Egypt's rulers. It was in this setting that we get the story of Moses being raised up to deliver Israel from bondage, a type of what was to come in the future through the Savior's atonement, and also of Ephraim's role in reclaiming scattered Israel from their fallen state (see Jeremiah 31: 6-22; 27-34).

Shortly before Israel's death he called Joseph to bring his sons Ephraim and Manasseh before him and then adopted them into his family, giving them equal blessings with his own sons. He designated Ephraim as the birthright son, even though he was the younger of the two, and made him authorized and responsible for governing the house of Israel. On him would rest the responsibility of gathering the scattered members of the house of Israel in the last days (see Genesis 48: 1-22).

23. And the Lord said unto her, Two nations are in thy womb,
and two manner of people shall be separated from thy
bowels; and the one people shall be stronger than the other
people; and the elder shall serve the younger.
—Genesis 25:23

CHAPTER 2

THE BIRTHRIGHT
A CONTINUATION OF THE
COVENANT

The story of Joseph and his brothers illustrates the parameters that the Lord sets when we are dealing with him in a covenant relationship. It also can be an insight to us as we strive to become part of his chosen family (i.e. covenant sons and daughters of God). By examining the history of the posterity of Israel's sons (the tribes of Israel), we uncover the Father's plan for the salvation of his children on this earth.

We must first start with the story of Jacob and Esau. Jacob (or Israel as his name was changed to by God [Genesis 32: 28]), had traveled to the homeland of his mother Rebekah to find a wife. His brother Esau had chosen not to marry in the covenant, but rather had married two women of Canaanite descent. It had been revealed to Rebekah, their mother, while they were still in her womb that Jacob not Esau was to inherit the birthright (see Genesis 25: 20-23). Esau sold the birthright to Jacob for a mess of pottage (see Genesis 25: 27-34). In this, his actions spoke louder than his words. For it is plain to see from this account that he had little regard for the things of the Spirit in his general deportment. It also seems quite obvious that his word didn't mean much to him. As the account tells us, upon the request of his father Isaac, Esau went out to hunt venison for the intended purpose of making his father a savory meal prior to receiving the birthright blessing at his hand. If he

7

fully intended on going through with it, his deal with Israel for the pottage was done without any real intention of following through on his part. At any rate Rebekah saw to it that Jacob got the blessing. She overheard Isaac telling Esau to get the meal for him, and took matters into her own hands. Upon killing a kid from the flock, she prepared Isaac's favorite meal and sent it in with Jacob.

The account appears a bit suspect for a couple of reasons. One, she put animal skins on his arms and neck to make him appear to be as hairy as Esau. Unless Esau was a relative of "Sasquatch" it is doubtful that a person, blind or not would think it was the hair of a man. And secondly, you can't fool a prophet of God acting under the inspiration of the spirit in a blessing. The fact that Isaac knew he gave the blessing to the right son seems evident when he calls Jacob in before sending him back to Laban's abode for a wife. Prior to Jacob's departure, Isaac again blesses him with the blessings of the Abrahamic covenant, and reaffirms his position as the birthright son. These are hardly the actions of a patriarch who had been taken in a plot to unrighteously steal a blessing, and a position of that magnitude. He would have been totally justified in revoking the afore-given blessing, and replacing it with a cursing of condemnation, which he did not do. From his actions it appears that he was totally comfortable with things as they were and therefore left them as they were (see Genesis 27:1-38; 28:1-5).

Upon realizing that he had truly lost the birthright blessing: "Esau hated Jacob because of the blessing wherewith his father blessed him: and Esau said in his heart, The days of mourning for my father are at hand; then will I slay my brother (Genesis 27: 41). Rebekah heard of it and warned Jacob of Esau's wrath, so Jacob left Canaan and traveled to the land of Haran to seek a wife among the family of his mother's brother. He asked for her hand, and a deal was struck for her dowry. A dowry was normally supplied by the father of the groom and was given to ensure that the wife would be cared for in the event of the untimely demise of the husband, or if he were to prove negligent in the fulfillment of his duties as her confidant and provider. The woman he chose was Rachel the daughter of Laban.

In the case of unfaithfulness on the wife's part, she would forfeit the dowry to her husband as compensation for her betrayal. The usual amount of the dowry was three years wages, and if the groom's father could not provide it, the prospective husband could work to do so. Such was the case with Jacob. A deal was struck whereby he agreed to work for Laban for seven years for the right to marry her. This he did willingly, "And they seemed but a few days to him, because of the great love that he had for her" (see Genesis 29:15-20). At last the dowry was paid and the time for their marriage arrived.

The marriage ceremony was performed, and Jacob rejoiced... until the next morning when he discovered a tradition his new father-in-law had conveniently forgot to inform him of. It was customary for the eldest to marry before her younger sisters, and Rachel had an older sister, Leah. It was this sister not Rachel that Laban had married off to Jacob. Just how he was able to pull it off successfully is open to speculation. Perhaps it was because it was dark, and her face was veiled. She also could have been similar in build. Or maybe in all of the emotion and commotion of the marriage and subsequent celebration, and because such a move on Laban's part may never have occurred to him, he wasn't too observant. But the fact remained that he was married to Leah and the marriage had been consummated.

When he emerged the next morning from his tent Jacob must have been fuming. Seven long years of hard labor had turned into a nightmare of major proportions. What would happen now? What of his love for his chosen Rachel?...Enter again the doctrine of plurality of wives. Once again God sanctioned the marrying of a man to more than one woman. As Jacob approached his new father-in-law with this question, Laban was quick with the solution. Give her (Leah) her honeymoon, and let her feel like a wife for a week and then you can marry Rachel too, was his reply. Just one catch though, Jacob would have to stay and work for another seven years for that privilege. Unlike what most of us would probably have done, Jacob agreed to the terms. And unlike his father-in-law he lived by them. Thus it was that the most significant family in the history of mankind had its humble beginnings (see Genesis 29:21-30).

27. *And he said unto him, What is thy name? And he said, Jacob.*
28. *And he said, Thy name shall be called no more Jacob, but Israel: for as a prince hast thou power with God and with men, and hast prevailed.*

—Genesis 32:27-28

CHAPTER 3
THE HOUSE OF ISRAEL

God established His covenant with Jacob, and gave unto him a new name, Israel (Genesis 32: 24-28). God then began to bless Israel with a large posterity. His chosen wife Rachel had her womb closed up, and try as she might she could not conceive and give him children. A woman in that time looked upon the ability to give her husband offspring as the primary purpose of her life. Of particular importance to them were sons who could carry on the father's name, and to whom he could pass on his inheritance. The fact that Rachel couldn't give Israel seed was very distressing to her.

Meanwhile back at the tent, her sister Leah was lengthening her lead in the baby derby, having not only baby after baby, but son after son! On top of that she seems to have been using this advantage over Rachel as a way to win Israel's heart. Well, as you might imagine a genuine rivalry evolved from these circumstances and got so intense that finally out of what was surely a total sense of frustration, Rachel gave her personal handmaid Bilhah to her husband as a concubine for the purpose of raising up seed unto her, as Sarah had done with Abraham. Since Bilhah was considered her property, the children born to her would be Rachel's as well. This was apparently a common practice of the day. From this, his third wife, Israel was given two more sons.

But the story was far from over, for Leah had left bearing children, and when she saw that Rachel was using her handmaid to obtain offspring, she was jealous and decided that two

11

could play that game, so she gave Israel her own handmaid Zilpah, who also bore Israel two more sons. God indeed seemed serious in fulfilling that portion of the Abraham covenant, which promised an infinite posterity! The rivalry between the two sisters over the graces of their husband had now reached epic proportions! An account is shared with us of a bartering session between the two. It involved mandrakes, a fruit that was traditionally thought to insure fertility and conception. Rachel asked Leah for some mandrakes that her son had given her, no doubt to try and reenter the competition in the baby sweepstakes. The payment for the mandrakes was to be Israel himself. This leads one to wonder why Leah had really left childbearing. Could it be that Israel had taken up his primary residence with Rachel? It certainly would appear so, because in the account we read that Rachel agrees to the deal, and Israel returns to spend time with Leah once again (see Genesis 30: 14-17).

Well, back to the story. Leah again conceives and bears Israel two more sons and then a daughter, which they named Dinah. Meanwhile, the Lord finally answers Rachel's pleadings with a son of her own. It must have been a blessed event the day that this son was born. After so many years of barrenness and discouragement, he finally had a son of his beloved Rachel. They named him Joseph.

In time Rachel would bring one more son into the world, but not without a cost. As Israel and his family sojourned in the wilderness Rachel went into hard labor, and after a valiant struggle she delivered another son. But as fate would have it, that struggle proved to be too much for her mortal body, and she paid with the ultimate sacrifice, her life. The thing that she had lived and pleaded for had cost her life itself. Israel named this son Benjamin, and mourned her death.

Joseph and Benjamin were all he had left of his chosen sweetheart. True he still had three other wives, whom he must have grown to love as well, but Rachel . . . she was the one that he had truly loved with all his heart. Because of this special love Israel had for her, Joseph her first born held an equally special place in his heart, and his life. As a result he probably protected, and perhaps even babied this young son of his old age. Because of this favoritism, resentment and jealously began to grow in his older brother's hearts toward him (see Genesis 37: 3-5; 11).

Imagine, if you can, that you have a younger sibling who was "so good that he/she just really irritated you." Imagine also, how you would feel if your parents always favored them, and if it seemed that they could do no wrong; that it seemed as if everything you did wrong was used against you as being a bad example. Your parents then leave town and place that younger sibling in charge of you. Everything you do has to be approved by them first. How would you like that arrangement? How would you react to their "constructive criticism?" Would you obey their every command, or would you be looking for the first opportunity to humble them a little?

Israel gave Joseph a special coat. This coat symbolized that he would be the birthright son, therefore not only getting a double portion of their father's inheritance financially, but of more importance, placing him in charge as the patriarch of the family (see Genesis 37:3). His will and word would be binding. The older brothers took exception to this "obvious" favoritism, and took every opportunity to pick on their younger sibling. Then there came the dreams! As if it weren't enough with him parading around all the time in his special little authoritative coat, Joseph then began having dreams about ruling over his brothers. One would think that after all of the persecution he was receiving at the hands of his brothers, Joseph would keep anything that would seem to further irritate them to himself. But for whatever reason, Joseph chose to tell them of his dreams. This move doesn't seem to have been a very intelligent one, and it apparently so infuriated his older brothers that they began to plot against his very life. Even his father seems to have wondered somewhat about the whole thing, but he accepted its premise nonetheless.

It was under these circumstances that Israel, one day, sent Joseph into the field to find his brothers and take them fresh supplies. As the young man (age 17) approached his older brothers, their jealousy and deriding finally got the best of them. The original plan was to kill him and see what came of his dreams of ruling over them. But Reuben stepped forward and said he would not allow such a thing. This was an interesting gesture on his part, because he was the one who had been supplanted by Joseph for the birthright, he being the oldest son of the family.

As a result of his protests, the brothers decided instead to throw him down the shaft of an old abandoned well. This seems to have satisfied Reuben, who then apparently left the others, planning to return and secretly remove his younger brother from the well and deliver him back to the safety of their father.

Meanwhile the gravity of their situation probably began to occur to the other brothers. They had put themselves in quite a predicament. Once they had thrown him into the well and threatened his life, they would have to deal with their father's wrath. But at least if they left Joseph in the well he would die on his own, and they wouldn't have to be physically involved in his demise. As they were deliberating on the matter, an opportune twist of fate presented itself.

A group of Ishmaelite traders happened by on their way to Egypt. Judah was the one who seems to have had the bright idea of selling their problem to the travelers. Why not kill two birds with one stone he thought, get rid of the troublesome Joseph once and for all, and make a little profit in the process. It doesn't appear that he had much difficulty convincing his brothers to go along with his idea, because we read that he was drawn out of the well and sold to the Ishmaelites for twenty pieces of silver, the common cost of a slave his age (Genesis 37:18-35).

With the dirty deed done, the remaining brothers set out to cover their tracks. They killed a goat, and smeared the blood on Joseph's treasured coat, which they had removed from him and kept when they sold him. Meanwhile, Reuben had returned to the pit to rescue his younger sibling, and not finding him there, he panicked. He approached his brothers with his tale of woe, and was shown the coat, torn and bloody. Whether he was told the truth of Joseph's whereabouts is uncertain. Knowing Reuben's strong feelings against harming him in the first place, it's doubtful that they would have fessed up to their crime to him. Maybe it was a sense of responsibility being the oldest, or perhaps because of not wanting to hurt his father, but whatever the reason, it seems clear that Reuben's intention was to protect the younger Joseph from harm, at all cost. And it also appears that the brothers pulled the "wool" of the slain goat over his eyes, as well as those of their father, Israel, who upon hearing the news mourned in sackcloth and ashes for his lost son.

It would be twenty long years until any of them would know the truth about what happened to the brother they had betrayed into the hands of the Egyptians. Imagine the burden those brothers must have carried all those many long years, watching the grief of their aged father, refusing to be comforted over the loss of the firstborn of his beloved Rachel, who herself had long since gone home to the world of spirits. I also wonder how many sleepless nights those brothers must have had lying in the darkness of the night, pondering what they had done, and wondering what had become of their long lost brother. There must have been accusing voices in the quiet of those endless nights, penetrating eyes that seemed to always be watching them, and the image of the young Joseph pleading with them to help him. Surely guilt would be their constant companion for the rest of their lives. Was he dead, or was he a slave being beaten and abused by some taskmaster in the brick pits of Egypt? They surely would never have known had it not been for the character of this uncommon young man.

9.   *There is none greater in this house than I; neither hath he kept back any thing from me but thee, because thou art his wife: how then can I do this great wickedness, and sin against God?*

—Genesis 39:9

CHAPTER 4
JOSEPH, A CHOSEN VESSEL

Being thrown in a dark, empty cavern and left there in solitary confinement would in itself be enough of a gut wrenching experience, but to have been deposited there by his own brothers must have been almost more than the teen-aged Joseph could bear. Especially when you take into consideration his charitable nature. Why would those he loved so much do such a thing to their little brother? He may even have thought that they were just putting him in the well to teach him a lesson, that after some time to feel some fear they would draw him out and give him another stern warning about encroaching on their rights. However, reality must surely have set in as the money changed hands, and Joseph was taken forcefully from their presence.

Abandoned by his family, and sold into slavery in a strange land, Joseph was taken from the land of his birth to begin a sojourn that would not only spare the house of Israel physically, but would literally make possible the fulfillment of the covenant made by God with Abraham; that through his seed all of the nations and families of the earth would be blessed.

There are a number of reactions one might have when thrust into this particular type of situation as this teenager was. The most common being bitterness and rebellion, not only against his brothers, but also more particularly against God Himself for not sparing him the ordeal of bondage and heartache. However this young man was anything but common, as the residents of Egypt were, in time, to discover.

16

Perhaps the first to sense this difference was Potiphar, the captain of the guard who purchased him, and gave him the assignment of being a steward in his own house.

The Egyptian rulers at the time of Joseph were apparently the Hyksos people. The ancient historian Manetho called them the shepherd-kings. They were a Semitic people from the lands north and east of Egypt. If indeed these people were in control, that might explain why Joseph was able to quickly gain such a degree of favor with Potiphar. It will also make the rest of this amazing story a lot easier to comprehend as well. Manetho also alluded to the fact that the Egyptians bitterly hated the Hyksos that had overthrown and dominated them. At any rate, Joseph served Potiphar faithfully and diligently, in any task that was assigned to him.

Potiphar's wife (who it seems was lacking a bit in character, and a whole lot in common sense!) appears to have taken a special interest in Joseph. Something about this peculiar young man caught her fancy, and she openly pursued his affections. Joseph somehow managed to keep his distance from her, and maintain his moral purity. But one day while he went about his normal tasks in Potiphar's house, she became particularly aggressive in her pursuit, and openly propositioned him, to the extent of trying to pull him close to her. He stoutly resisted her advances, and backed up his refusal by reminding her of all the trust her husband had placed in him. He rehearsed to her how his master had given everything he had to him, except her, because she was his wife.

At this point it would stand to reason that this rationale would be followed up with a profession of loyalty to Potiphar for his kindness. However . . . not so. Instead, he made a statement that revealed the true character of this exceptional young man. He said, "How can I do this great wickedness and sin against God?" (see Genesis 39:9). As good as Potiphar had been to him, there was still a far stronger passion which drove him to resist such an advance. It was a deep love and sense of loyalty for his "real Master." At his refusal, Potiphar's wife grabbed at his clothing in an attempt to pull him near her.

Joseph reacted in the only way he could. He "got himself out," or in other words . . . he ran! This may not have been the most romantic response, but it was definitely the wisest he could have made! So down the path he ran, loincloth and all, right to prison! Joseph's integrity had cost him his freedom temporarily, for infuriated (and perhaps humiliated) by the rebuff given to her by Joseph, Mrs. Potiphar cried foul! She accused Joseph of the ultimate impropriety, sexual harassment! Citing his pilfered clothing as evidence, she demanded that justice be meted out.

Now bear in mind that Potiphar was a very powerful man in Egypt. The Hebrew phrase, which is translated as "captain of the guards," literally means "chief of the butchers or slaughterers." If he was indeed the royal executioner who executed the capital sentences ordered by the king, Joseph was in deep trouble. This makes the sentence given him by Potiphar such an interesting one. It should have been instant death, no questions asked, for such an accusation made against him. But instead, Potiphar gave him a prison sentence. I wonder whom he trusted more, Joseph or his wife? I'll leave that one up to you to figure out! Perhaps he knew his wife. Maybe this wasn't the first time she'd had a problem in the area of faithfulness. At any rate, Joseph probably had to be given some kind of a sentence in order to save face with the people of Egypt. But it doesn't appear that Potiphar was convinced of Joseph's guilt sufficiently to sentence him to death.

So Joseph went to prison, and again must have wondered why this was all happening to him. Once again he could have blamed his circumstances on his God. But, as seemed to always be the case with him, he just went about making the best of whatever circumstances were dealt to him. During his stay in prison he was elevated to a kind of "keeper of the prison" status.

During this time he also made acquaintance with two of Pharaoh's former chief employees, the chief baker, and chief butler, who themselves were "doing time" for some supposed impropriety. They had both been troubled by their dreams.

Joseph offered to interpret them, and had both interpretations come to pass. The butler was restored to his former office, and the baker was hanged, just as Joseph had prophesied. So impressed was the butler by Joseph's insight, that he promised to tell Pharaoh of him upon his reinstatement. However, as is often the case, the promise went unfulfilled. And Joseph spent another two years behind bars before circumstances arose which would jog the butler's memory.

It so happened that the Pharaoh himself began to have a recurring dream of his own. He summoned the wise men and soothsayers of his kingdom to aid him in deciphering its meaning to him. After they had tried without success to do so, the butler remembered Joseph, and upon being told of a Hebrew slave that had the ability to do such things, Pharaoh summoned him to his court. The content of the dream was rehearsed, and the meaning of it requested of this Hebrew. Being aided by the Spirit of God, Joseph interpreted it as a warning to Pharaoh of what God would shortly bring to pass. Seven years of plenty would be followed by seven more years of famine in the land. Food was to be stored and laid away during the years of plenty in preparation for the lean ones to follow. Pharaoh was also advised by Joseph to select a man of wisdom to be in charge of overseeing such a plan. So impressed was the Pharaoh by the stature of the man that stood before him, that he selected Joseph as that man.

After enduring the better part of two decades as a slave and a prisoner, Joseph became the second most powerful man in the world. Only Pharaoh himself would have more power than he was given. The long years of dedicated patience had finally begun to pay major dividends for the man destined to be the head of the tribes of Israel.

64. *And the Lord shall scatter thee among all people, from the one end of the earth even unto the other; and there thou shalt serve other gods, which neither thou nor thy fathers have known, even wood and stone.*

—Deuteronomy 28:64

10. *Hear the word of the Lord, O ye nations, and declare it in the isles afar off, and say, He that scattered Israel will gather him, and keep him, as a shepherd doth his flock.*
11. *For the Lord hath redeemed Jacob, and ransomed him from the hand of him that was stronger than he.*

—Jeremiah 31:10-11

CHAPTER 5

THE SCATTERING AND GATHERING OF ISRAEL

Sometime after the famine began, Israel and his posterity began to feel its effects. Word had come to the elderly patriarch that the Egyptians had vast supplies that they were willing to sell. Finally, he instructed his older sons to travel to Egypt to buy grain. Only Benjamin would not make the journey. Israel was bound and determined not to let his last son from Rachel perish, as had Joseph some twenty years earlier. No, this journey would have to be done without his youngest son.

The brothers arrived in Egypt, money in hand, to beg for sustenance from the great Zapthnath-Paaneah (Joseph's Egyptian name), the mighty one of Egypt. Within his hands he held their hope for life. Little did they know that this mighty one that they bowed themselves before, was none other than their little brother Joseph, who twenty years earlier they had sold into slavery because he had foretold of this very event. The emotions that Joseph must have experienced would be next to impossible to imagine. What would you do if placed in a similar situation? Would you revel in the moment of power, and exact revenge?

20

Would you let them feel the bitter sting of slavery also? I'm sure a flood of emotions filled his heart as he looked upon their helpless state before him. Had they changed during the past twenty years? Was there remorse in their hearts for their cowardly deed of so long ago? Joseph desired to know, but how?

A test by which the state of their hearts could be known was devised. Joseph had them thrown into jail on accusations as spies coming to see the weakness of Egypt. Despite there protestations of innocence, he had them incarcerated. Then just as quickly as they were jailed they were freed, except Simeon, who was to remain in jail until the rest of the brothers returned, this time with the last remaining brother, Benjamin. They were given their provisions and sent on their way.

Relieved and probably somewhat confused, they journeyed toward Canaan and the tent of their father, with the provisions, but minus one more brother. Joseph had secretly instructed his servant to put each brother's money back in the mouth of his sack.

Upon the brothers' return, they opened their sacks and found their money in the mouth of each. Their first reaction, it seems from the record, was that God was punishing them for what they had done to Joseph so many years earlier (see Genesis 42: 21-24).

It also appears from this reaction that they had probably done some serious soul searching over the years, and their consciences had become a bit more acute from the guilt they surely must have suffered. They probably hoped that the food they had obtained would last them for the duration of the famine. How would they explain the retention of the payment for their grain?

Perhaps it was because of the pain and shame that Simeon had exacted upon Israel with the slaughter of the men at Shechem, that Israel reacted the way he did when told that he had been left behind in jail. And it most assuredly had to do with Benjamin being the only remaining son of Rachel. But Israel refused at first to even entertain the thought of risking his beloved Benjamin to save the freedom of his elder brother (see Genesis 42-43). It was only when they needed more grain that he finally relented.

Judah stepped forward, and offered the lives of his own sons if he did not return with Benjamin. Though their lives in no way would be able to atone for the possible loss of Benjamin, Israel probably realized that there was no other alternative if they wanted food for their survival. So he relented, and allowed his beloved Benjamin to return with them to Egypt, at the same time not realizing that he was in reality in the process of reuniting his long separated family. Upon arriving back in Egypt they were once again incarcerated, and left to ponder their former lack of compassion. They were then released and led to a banquet in Joseph's personal quarters. After a few more tests, Joseph revealed himself to them, whereupon they fell prostrate on the floor before him. In fear, they begged his forgiveness, but were informed by Joseph that there were no hard feelings. Joseph then sent for his aging father to bring the rest of the family to the land of Goshen where they would be well provided for, through the duration of the famine, and beyond.

This strange sequence of events resulted in Israel's people living in the land of Egypt for some 400 years. However, more importantly, it clearly established Joseph as the head of the tribes of Israel. Thus, the birthright blessing, which was given to him years earlier was about to be put into force.

Before Israel died he desired to adopt Joseph's two sons, Ephraim and Manasseh, into his family. He requested that Joseph bring them to him. Joseph did so and positioned Ephraim on his left hand, and Manasseh on his right. The scriptures record the significance of being on the right hand of God as those who will inherit eternal life with him in his kingdom. The account states that the elderly Israel, who, by the way, was now blind, crossed his hands and laid his right hand on the head of Ephraim, not on his elder brother. When Joseph attempted to correct the supposed error, his father informed him that he knew very well what he was doing, and that Ephraim, not Manasseh, was to inherit the birthright, and thus the ecclesiastical authority over the tribes of Israel. The children of Israel remained in Egypt until Moses led them out of bondage, and into the land of Canaan by Joshua. I quote from the *Encyclopedia Judaica Jr.*: "In the same way that priests lift their hands in blessing, so parents place their hands on the heads of their children when they bless them. For example, in the Bible, Jacob blessed his grandsons, Ephraim and Manasseh, by placing his hands on their heads. Placing the hands on another person is symbolic not only of transferring blessing but also of passing on authority. In Talmudic times, scholars received their rabbinic ordination through the symbolic act of placing of the hands (known as Semikhah)."

In modern Judaism, there is a powerful cultural and legendary history of Joseph and his future role. Some of these excerpts provide insight regarding the modern Joseph the Jews are still anticipating. Again I quote from the *Encyclopedia Judaica Jr.*:

> "Based on the famous story of Joseph and his brothers, the Talmud warns against favoring one child over another . . . jealousy is considered such a serious evil that it is mentioned in the Ten Commandments where the tenth commandment is an outright prohibition of envy. The Rabbis of the Talmud developed the philosophy that a truly rich man is one who is happy with his portion in life and does not envy others. According to the Talmud, the Messiah will be a descendant of the house of David and will be preceded by a secondary Messiah from the house of Joseph. When the Chief Rabbi, Avraham Hakohen Kook, was appointed in Palestine in the 1920's, he was asked if the Jews could now build the temple (destroyed since year 70 A.D.). His response was that the priestly rights were gone and referred to the great 12th century Rabbi Moses Maimonides. Maimonides said, in effect, 'we are waiting for a Messiah Ben-Joseph, to him will be given the keys to the gathering of Israel, he will restore temple worship.'"

Apparently, even the Jews understand that the priesthood authority belongs to the tribe of Joseph. The chiasmus shows that the ancient Joseph saved his family and they did not know who he was. The latter-day Joseph is saving his brothers again (more foreign aid goes to Israel from the USA, the land of Joseph, than from all other countries combined), and they don't know that it is Joseph. In the meridian of time, there was

"One" who saved us all . . . and still most people don't recognize it" (Daniel Rona, *Holy Land and Jewish Insights*).

The history of Israel changed dramatically once the children of Israel arrived in the land of Canaan. Upon arriving there the land was divided into parcels and each tribe received its promised inheritance. That is, except for those of the tribe of Levi, who were dispersed among the other tribes in order to fulfill their priestly responsibilities as holders of the Levitical priesthood, or priesthood of Aaron. They were designated as the ones who would offer the sacrifices for the people, under the Law of Moses. The Levites were the only tribe allowed by God to hold his priesthood. They also officiated in the tabernacle, and were responsible for transporting the Ark of the Covenant. The tribes settled in Canaan and began to multiply in numbers, and in wickedness.

Before they ever entered the Promised Land they had been instructed by the Lord to destroy everything that lived and breathed, including women and children, and animals (see Deuteronomy 7: 1-5; Joshua 6: 21). As the Lord explained in Deuteronomy 7: 4, he didn't want them to have any idea of the wickedness that was going on in this new home of theirs. Israel didn't obey that advice, and, as a result, they did fall into the immoral practices of the inhabitants of the land. Because of their immorality and wickedness, the Lord raised up prophets, and sent them unto the children of Israel to warn them to repent or they would be destroyed. In approximately 925 B.C., because of the heavy taxes that King Solomon and, then, Rehoboam had levied on the children of Israel, they revolted. Ten of the tribes formed what was referred to as the Northern Kingdom. These included all of the tribes but Judah, and part of the tribe of Benjamin. They set up their headquarters at Shechem in Samaria, and soon fell into total apostasy. With Ephraim, the birthright son, being the dominant tribe, they were also referred to as Ephraim, or as Israel.

The Southern Kingdom was comprised mainly of the tribe of Judah, and included the descendants of King David, and that line of royalty. They were referred to as Judah, and had their headquarters in the city of Jerusalem. Modern day descendants of these people still inhabit that area and are called Jews. In the book of Genesis as stated earlier, after having adopted Joseph's sons as his own and making them each a tribe of equal standing, Israel called them all together and wished to give them all a special priesthood blessing before he died (see Genesis 49:1-29).

Upon closer inspection of these blessings it becomes crystal clear that two of those blessings stand out far above the rest. They are the ones given to Judah, and Joseph, bearing in mind that Joseph's posterity from that time forward would be two tribes, not one. There really is no "Tribe of Joseph" after this point in the scriptures, just Manasseh, and Ephraim the birthright son. Joseph died in Egypt and his bones were carried out of that land, into the land of Canaan by Moses during the exodus (see Joshua 24:32).

When the Northern Kingdom went into apostasy, the Lord sent them such prophets as Elijah, Amos and others. Despite their ministries Israel sank deeper into the worship of Baal, with its evil and immoral rituals. As a result of their sin and disobedience, the Lord allowed them to be conquered by Assyria, who at that time was the most feared and powerful kingdom on earth. They were conquered and subsequently carried away captive into Assyria (see 2 Kings 17). They became known as the "lost ten tribes."

Since the day of their captivity they have not returned to their homeland, but they have become a part of folklore, and their whereabouts have led to a plethora of speculation. The Bible prophesies of their dramatic return when they are ready to obey the gospel that they formerly rejected (see Isaiah 11: 10-16; Jeremiah 3:18, 16:14-21).

1. *How doth the city sit solitary, that was full of people! how is she become as a widow! she that was great among the nations, and princess among the provinces, how is she become solitary!*

—*Lamentations 1:1*

CHAPTER 6
THE FALL OF JUDAH

Now let's turn our attention to the remaining kingdom, that of Judah. Because of taxation and jealousy that existed between the tribes of Ephraim and Judah, the house of Israel divided. The Southern Kingdom included the tribe of Judah, and the greater part of the tribe of Benjamin. On the whole, it remained more faithful to the worship of Jehovah than had the Northern Kingdom of Israel, though it did struggle with problems of its own from time to time. Because it had some very righteous kings such as Hezekiah, that led the people in the righteous ways of their fathers, they managed to stay intact for some 135 years after the Northern Kingdom was carried away into captivity. But as was the case with Israel, they too, eventually, slipped into apostasy, and likewise paid the ultimate price for their rebellion. We'll continue with the story during the reign of King Zedekiah.

Not many years after the Assyrians had captured Israel, and carried her away, its empire began to crumble. Up and coming powers, the Chaldeans, and the Babylonians, were beginning to flex their muscles, and they had Assyria in their collective cross hairs. In 609 B.C., King Nabopolassar, in league with Egypt and Media, captured the city of Nineveh, the capital city of the Assyrian Empire. Babylon then became the dominant power, and like the Assyrians before them, used a strategy of conquest and deportation to get the upper hand on their rivals. When Nabopolassar died, his son Nebuchadnezzar inherited the ruling power for the Babylonian Empire. It was under his shrewd leadership that Babylon grew to the height of its majesty and greatness.

When he conquered a country he would get rid of those who would interfere with, or challenge his domain. He would then take the brightest, most gifted young people of their land and use them to his greatest advantage. He would use these slaves to build his city, and quickly turned it into the greatest city in the world. The wealth of the world flowed through its coffers as a result of his conquests and commerce. But it wasn't just its material wealth that set Babylon apart from the rest of the world. For, as is so often the case with wealth and luxury, the morals of its society decayed in direct proportion with its accumulation of wealth. So much so in fact, that the Bible writers ever after referred to Babylon as the symbol of ultimate worldliness and wickedness. The Apostle John refers to it as being "The great whore of all the earth," and the "mother of harlots" (see Revelation 17:1,5). It was to this kingdom that Judah found itself under servitude. Of anyone under heaven, they should have understood the end result of wickedness. They had watched as the Northern Kingdom disintegrated and was scattered at the hands of the Assyrians. Judah itself had been delivered from the hands of the Assyrian army, because they gave heed to the pleadings of the prophet Isaiah (see 2 Kings 17-18). The Lord is no respecter of persons, and Judah should have known that if the Northern Kingdom had been destroyed because of its wickedness, if they were no better themselves, they would most surely face a similar fate.

But Judah was a proud people, and it failed to read the handwriting on the wall. After Assyria was toppled, and as Babylon sought to establish itself, the pressures on the Southern Kingdom of Judah were lessened. Rather than humble themselves in gratitude for their eased burdens, the people became all the more deeply entrenched in idolatry. In fact, even more than their sister to the north had been (see 2 Kings 21:9).

It was in this state of wickedness that Judah lost her divine promise of protection from Jehovah. The Lord sent his prophets to warn the people, as he always does, of their extreme wickedness, and subsequent impending doom, if they didn't reverse their slide. Up and coming Babylon, hungry for power, stood waiting to exact God's punishment upon them. Indeed, it was just the power that it would take to bring rebellious Judah to her knees.

After the time of King Hezekiah, and for approximately the next 120 years, the Kingdom of Judah found itself in a tailspin of wickedness and abominations that culminated in the destruction of Jerusalem, and deportation of its people at the hands of Babylon. Judah was caught in the middle of a power struggle between super powers Egypt and Babylonia, and without the divine guidance of Jehovah, its kings made critical mistakes, which eventually sealed its doom.

Manasseh, the son of Hezekiah turned Judah to idolatry, building altars for Baal in the house of the Lord (the Temple). Because of the evil, which he introduced into Judah, the Lord sent prophets to warn the people of their impending doom should they not repent and return to him (2 Kings 21:1-16). Following the reign of Manasseh, his son Amon also reigned in wickedness, as did his father. He was slain by his servants in his own house. This act of treachery lead the people of the land to slay all those who had conspired against Amon, and then to install Josiah, his son, in his stead (see 2 Kings 21:19-24).

Josiah was a righteous man, and seems to have been the one bright spot in the consuming darkness surrounding Judah during this bleak period of its history. Josiah reigned for 31 years in Jerusalem. He commissioned Hilkiah, the high priest to make repairs to the temple. During this renovation Hilkiah discovered the Book of the Law (scriptures) and brought them to Josiah. He had Shaphan the scribe read its words to him, and his blood ran cold with what they said.

Being raised by an idolatrous father, I'm sure he had no idea of the extent of the trouble his father and grandfather had brought upon Judah, and just how close the Lord was to bringing down his punishments on them. He then asked Hilkiah and others who may have been somewhat more familiar with prayer, to inquire of the Lord for him as to their status. He may not have been schooled in the things of God, but it appears that he was a righteous man, from his words upon hearing the words of God.

> Go ye, enquire of the Lord for me, and for the people, and for all Judah, concerning the words of this book that is found: for great is the wrath of the Lord that is kindled against us, because our fathers have not hearkened unto the words of this book, to do according unto all that which is written concerning us (2 Kings 22:13).

The word of the Lord came back to him that Jerusalem was on a collision course with destruction, but because he had hearkened to the light that he had been given, and humbled himself before God, it would be postponed until he had passed from this life (see 2 Kings 22:14-20).

The twenty-third chapter begins with Josiah taking action to undo the evil in which they were so deeply steeped. He started by having the scriptures read to the people, and followed that up by having them enter into a covenant to keep the commandments they contained. His next action was to overturn the worship of false gods among them. He removed the Sodomites, and had all of the idolatrous priests put to death. He finalized his efforts by reestablishing the observance of the Passover.

> And like unto him was there no king before him, that turned to the Lord with all his heart, and with all his soul, and with all his might, according to all the law of Moses; neither after him arose there any like him (2 Kings 23:25).

But the fate of Judah was set, and the Lord turned not his fierce anger away from Judah. One righteous man does not a nation make, and such was the case here. We pick up the story in the twenty-ninth verse of chapter twenty-three. We read that "Pharaoh—Nechoh, King of Egypt went up against the King of Assyria to the river Euphrates: and King Josiah went against him;" and he (the king) slew him (Josiah) at Megiddo."

Josiah's servants brought him from Megiddo in a chariot and buried him in his own sepulchre. They then anointed his son

Jehoahaz to succeed him. Almost immediately this new monarch returned to the idolatry of his fathers. The final phase of their journey had been put into motion, for without the Spirit of the Lord to guide him as it did his father, he was:

> Put in bands at Riblah in the land of Hamath, that he might not reign in Jerusalem; and he put the land to a tribute of an hundred talents of silver, and a talent of gold (2 Kings 23:33)

And Pharaoh-Nechoh made Eliakim the son of Josiah the king and changed his name to Jehoiakim, "and he took Jehoahaz away: and he came to Egypt, and he died there" (2 Kings 23:34). Thus in approximately 609 B.C., Jehoiakim and Judah were put under tribute to Egypt. Jehoiakim reigned for some 11 years, and he continued in the evil ways of his fathers. Upon his death his son Jehoiachin reigned in his stead, who . . .(you guessed it) followed in the evil footsteps of his father. In the eighth year of Jehoiachin's reign King Nebuchadnezzar came against Jerusalem and besieged it. He looted the temple, and carried all of its treasures therein away into Babylon.

> And he carried away all Jerusalem, and all the princes, and all the mighty men of valor, even ten thousand captives, and all the craftsmen and smiths: none remained, save the poorest sort of the people of the land.

> And he carried away Jehoiachin to Babylon, and the king's mother, and the king's wives, and his officers, and the mighty of the land, those carried he into captivity from Jerusalem to Babylon.

> And all the men of might, even seven thousand, all that were strong and apt for war, even them the king of Babylon brought captive to Babylon (2 Kings 24:14-16).

Then the king made Mattaniah, Jehoiachin's uncle, king in his stead, and changed his name to Zedekiah. He was a wicked man, and in essence a "Puppet King," doing everything Nebuchadnezzar told him to do. That is until the ninth year of his reign. It appears he was growing somewhat weary of paying tribute to Babylon, so he set out to see what he could do about changing all that. He was apparently trying to negotiate some sort of a deal to align Judah with Egypt, and thus get out from under Babylon's heavy hand. But it seems as though Nebuchadnezzar got wind of it.

> *And it came to pass in the ninth year of his reign, in the tenth month, in the tenth day of the month, that Nebuchadnezzar King of Babylon came, he, and all his host, against Jerusalem, and pitched against it; and they built forts against it round about. And the city was besieged unto the eleventh year of King Zedekiah. And on the ninth day of the fourth month the famine prevailed in the city, and there was no bread for the people of the land. And the city was broken up, and all the men of war fled by night by the way of the gate between two walls (2 Kings 25:1-4).*

Zedekiah fled the city, toward the plain. He was eventually overtaken, captured, and brought to Riblah, before the king.

> *And they slew the sons of Zedekiah before his eyes, and put out the eyes of Zedekiah, and bound him with fetters of brass, and carried him to Babylon (2 Kings 25:7).*

And in the fifth month, on the seventh day of the month, Nebuchadnezzar's forces stormed the city and laid it to waste. They burned the Temple, the King's house and every other great man's house, and carried anything they could find of any value away with them into Babylon. The Jews they didn't kill were carried away, and only the poor of the city did they leave behind to be vinedressers and husbandmen. All the wealth that Solomon had accumulated and placed in the temple was broken or melted down and carried away. Gold, silver, and all manner of precious stones and vessels were carried off.

And so it was that the once mighty city of Jerusalem, the one that King David had made into the pride of all Israel, was laid to ruin, and its inhabitants carried off into slavery. Just as their stiff-necked brethren to the north had fallen to the Assyrians, they too learned the price for forsaking the light, and seeking darkness, and the things of the world.

6. *The Lord said also unto me in the days of Josiah the king, Hast thou seen that which backsliding Israel hath done? she is gone up upon every high mountain and under every green tree, and there hath played the harlot.*
7. *And I said after she had done all these things, Turn thou unto me. But she returned not. And her treacherous sister Judah saw it.*
8. *And I saw, when for all the causes whereby backsliding Israel committed adultery I had put her away, given her a bill of divorce; yet her treacherous sister Judah feared not, but went and played the harlot also.*

—Jeremiah 3:6-8

CHAPTER 7
UNHEEDED WARNINGS FULFILLED

With the ten tribes lost, and the remaining tribes of Benjamin and Judah now taken captive into Babylon, the house of Israel was in dire straits. From this time forth the Bible mainly records the history of the house of Judah, since they were the dominant remaining tribe. It tells of King Cyrus of Persia eventually allowing the Jews to return and rebuild both the temple, and the city of Jerusalem. And brings us up to the advent of the birth and ministry of the promised Messiah, Jesus Christ. But much of the remaining Old Testament record, are writings of the prophets, that God sent to warn his chosen people, the House of Israel, to repent of their wickedness, and return to him.

Prophets such as Jeremiah, Daniel, Isaiah, Ezekiel, and others preached to deaf ears in their quest to bring the stiff-necked Jews to return to Jehovah. Not only did the people reject these inspired men's messages, but they also abused them both verbally and physically.

Jeremiah was one of the few prophets to actually live to see the fulfillment of his prophecies come to pass. I guess we could look at that as a mixed blessing. The downside being, that he actually witnessed the fall of Judah to the Babylonians. The Lord informed Jeremiah that: "I will hasten my word to perform it" (Jeremiah 1:12). We learn a very valuable doctrine from this great prophet concerning our status before coming to this earth. Jeremiah 1:4-5 is a powerful evidence of the pre-mortal existence of man. The Lord told him that he knew him before he was formed in his mother's womb.

Jeremiah was born in Anathoth, and prophesied from the 13th year of Josiah till after the fall of Judah, from 626-586 BC. After Josiah's death Jeremiah was virtually alone in his crusade against idolatry and immorality. Judah was steeped in self-deception, founded on superficial reforms (see Jeremiah 3:4-5; 8-10), and of fanatical confidence in the Lord's protection, and he preached against that false premise as well. He faced continuous opposition from practically every front, from the priests (see Jeremiah 20:2), mobs (see Jeremiah 26:8-9), his townsmen from Anathoth (see Jeremiah 11:19), the king (see Jer. 36:19), the general public (see Jeremiah 22:13; 36:23; 26:20), and even from the army (see Jeremiah 38:4).

Jeremiah uses powerful imagery in his description of the covenant relationship that Jehovah has with Israel. He describes the Messiah as the bridegroom, and the House of Israel (his church) as his bride. He then uses the example of an unfaithful wife as a way to describe what he feels when they turn away from their covenants they have made with him. In a marriage relationship, infidelity, the ultimate betrayal, is what he uses to describe those feelings of hurt and disappointment, from her playing the harlot with false gods (see Jeremiah 3:1, 6, 9, 14, & 20). He also suffered at the hands of the Jews in Jerusalem because of his teachings against them (see Jeremiah 18:18).

Pashur, the chief overseer of the temple, had Jeremiah beaten and placed in stocks (see Jeremiah 20:1-6). Finally, when Judah fell to Babylon, Jeremiah was carried away into Egypt by fleeing Jews who had escaped Babylon's conquest, and who according to tradition stoned him there. He suffered through Judah's punishment with them, and though he had prophesied of their demise, he also foretold of their eventual redemption in the last days.

As great as Israel viewed the deliverance of ancient Israel by Moses, Jeremiah spoke of their future latter-day deliverance as a far greater event. He also prophesied that in that day the Lord would send "hunters" and "fishers," to seek them out, and gather them from the countries whither he had driven them. And that Judah would return to her homeland, and dwell with them in safety and peace (see Jeremiah 16:14-21). In short, he foretold of the day the Jews would be redeemed from their lost and fallen state (see Jeremiah 3:12-19).

Isaiah preached in Jerusalem from around 740-701 B.C. He had great religious and political influence during Hezekiah's reign as king. In fact, he was his chief advisor. He is the most quoted of all the Old Testament prophets, by the Savior and the New Testament writers. His writings are deeply spiritual and Christ-centered. Isaiah's writings are dualistic in nature. He wrote of conditions in his day, as well as future events. Some of his prophecies have already been fulfilled, and the rest are yet to be. The bulk of his prophecies are about the coming of the Redeemer, both in his first appearance, and also of his second coming as the great King and deliverer of Israel, at the last day.

One of his major themes was that God couldn't help His covenant people unless they were true to their covenants that they had made with Him. That they will be scattered and smitten until the day comes that they will obey Him and keep His commandments.

But in the end, Israel will turn to Him, and they will be restored to the lands of their inheritance. He will, at last, fight their battles and deliver them from their enemies. He will reign in majesty in their midst, and He will be their God, and they will be His people in Zion. He begins his record with what is a prologue to the rest of it.

The first chapter of Isaiah reveals the apostate, corrupt, rebellious condition of Israel, and concludes with their redemption in the latter-days. He also speaks of the mission of the Savior (see Isaiah 7:14; 9:6-7; 11:1-5; 53:1-12; 61:1-3), and of events of the latter-days, when the gospel is restored and Israel is gathered (see Isaiah 2; 11; 12; 35). Chapters 47-66 deal with events in the final restoration of Israel, the cleansing of the earth, and the establishment of Zion, with the Lord dwelling among His people. Isaiah has long been a difficult book for many to read with any real deep level of understanding, for a number of reasons. One main obstacle is his literary style and extensive use of symbolism and imagery. Many of his prophecies are begun in his day, but not fulfilled until the latter-days. Consequently, many of them may have more than one fulfillment or application. He was truly a prophet of exceptional latter-day foresight, whose warnings would have saved the house of Judah much misery, had they been heeded.

Daniel was one of the bright young minds that Nebuchadnezzar imported from Jerusalem for his own purposes. As mentioned before, it was quite commonplace for conquering kings to carry away the most gifted people from the conquered nation to serve them.

Nothing is known of his parentage, though it appears that he may have been of royal descent. He, along with three others, refused to eat of the King's meat for fear of defilement (see Daniel 1:8-16). Chapters 2-4 and 5 are the story of how he won the favor of Nebuchadnezzar and Darius with his ability to interpret dreams, much as Joseph had done for Pharaoh, centuries earlier. Due to a plot to destroy him, by making it illegal for a person to pray to their God, Daniel was thrown into a den of lions, where he was miraculously spared, when an Angel from God closed the lion's mouths (see Daniel 6).

The book of Daniel teaches its readers the importance of being true to God, no matter what the cost, and of the blessings that will come from that true obedience. This book is to the Old Testament what the book of Revelation, recorded by John is to the New Testament, in that it prophesies of events that are yet to occur relative to the end of the world. It is possibly the oldest book of apocalyptic writings in the entire Bible.

There are additions to this record not included in the current canon of scripture, but can be read in the Apocrypha (see Latter-day Saint Bible Dictionary). Daniel also prophesies of a restoration of the true and living gospel to the earth in the latter-days, and describes it as a "stone, cut out of the mountain without hands," which will roll forth, consuming all other kingdoms, until it fills the whole earth, "and it shall stand forever" (see Daniel 2:44-45).

Ezekiel was a priest of Zadok, and was one of the captives carried away into Babylon along with Jehoiachin, by Nebuchadnezzar. He prophesied from 592-570 B.C. His writings can be grouped into three main ideas or divisions:

Prophecies of judgment against Judah (see Ezekiel 1-24); Prophecies of the restoration (see Ezekiel 25-39); and visions of the reconstruction of the temple and its worship (see Ezekiel 40-48).

Ezekiel was a man of many visions, and had much to say about the future restoration of the house of Israel, and the glorious advent of the millennial reign of the Lord. Of particular importance to us is the 37th chapter of his book. For it is here where the story of the birthright comes into full focus, and where the big picture finally begins to come into plain view. We will return to this chapter in Ezekiel for in-depth scrutinizing in Chapter Nine.

In summary then, the tribes of Israel had long been warned of what would happen to them if they failed to be obedient to the Lord's commandments. As early as Deuteronomy the Lord had been very specific in outlining his blessings for obedience (see Deuteronomy 28:1-14), and punishments for rebellion (see Deuteronomy 28:15-68; Leviticus 26). Isaiah 10:5 contains a solemn warning to the ten tribes of Israel that if they did not repent, the Lord would use Assyria as "the rod of mine anger." They failed to give heed to the Lord's warnings, and consequently the prophesied judgements came to pass. As a result, Judah would learn for itself that same lesson. Isaiah warned them of their downfall in chapter three verses one through

eight, and had tried to get them to understand the consequences of forming alliances with other nations for protection,
instead of repenting and looking to him for safety (see Isaiah
7:1-16). But, they too failed to heed the voice of the Lord
through his prophets, and likewise, reaped the rewards of their
rebellion.

6. *For thou art an holy people unto the Lord thy God: the Lord thy God hath chosen thee to be a special people unto himself, above all people that are upon the face of the earth.*

—*Deuteronomy 7:6*

CHAPTER 8

A CHOSEN LINEAGE SET APART

We've gone into great detail concerning the covenant that God established with Abraham, and its subsequent effect on his posterity and the world. Before proceeding with the tie that binds this special covenant lineage, let's recap what we've discovered about Israel.

Abraham was severely tested by the Lord to see if he would obey his voice . . . at all costs. He was asked to offer his only son from his chosen wife, Sarah, on an altar as proof of his dedication. Abraham had been raised in a culture where the people offered their children to false gods, but knew that God had promised him a posterity from that chosen line as numerous as the sands of the sea, or the stars in the heavens. Somehow, that promise would be fulfilled. He never had to carry through with this particular sacrifice. God provided a ram in the thicket as a proxy for Isaac. But this display of loyalty on Abraham's part was enough for the Lord to know what he was made of. The promise to Abraham would be validated through his faithfulness.

At Abraham's death the birthright covenant was carried forth through Isaac, again, through his own personal righteousness and obedience. From Isaac it would be bestowed upon Jacob, not Esau who was the eldest, because of Esau's unworthiness and Jacob's integrity and obedience. Esau married out of the covenant (chosen lineage), but as we remember, their mother Rebekah sought Isaac's approval and support in sending Jacob to her brother's house, in order to insure that he would marry within the chosen lineage.

What was so important about that family? Weren't there any good people in the world besides people in their particular family? Of course there were, but to truly understand the importance of it we need to look again at the covenant. It was with Abraham's seed that the covenant was made, and for whatever reason, God chose that specific family and designated it as the covenant line that all the inhabitants of the earth, past, present and future would have to join themselves with in order to obtain salvation. Thus it was vital to keep that lineage intact. In the book of Deuteronomy, when Israel was being led into the "land of their inheritance," God instructed "Israel" to destroy all of the Canaanites, and not to make any covenants with them. He then states:

> Neither shalt thou make marriages with them; thy daughter thou shalt not give unto his son, nor his daughter thou shalt not take unto thy son.

> For they will turn away thy son from following me, that they may serve other Gods: so will the anger of the Lord be kindled against you, and destroy you suddenly (Deuteronomy 7:3-4).

Why does God make such a request of a group of people? Are they that much better than everyone else around them? Are they supposed to look down their noses at anyone who isn't a member of their "Church?" To fully understand his reasoning, He explains:

> For thou art an holy people unto the Lord thy God: the Lord thy God hath chosen thee to be a special people unto himself, above all people that are upon the face of the earth. The Lord did not set his love upon you, nor choose you, because ye were more in number than any people; for ye were the fewest of all people. But because the Lord loved you, and because he would keep the oath which he had sworn unto your fathers, hath the Lord brought you out with a mighty hand, and redeemed you out of the house of bondmen, from the hand of Pharaoh, king of Egypt (Deuteronomy 7:6-8).

There we have it, for whatever reason, the Lord had chosen this particular lineage to establish His Church through. And it was to be through them that He would choose to extend His blessings and covenants to all the inhabitants of the earth. On the surface it might appear that this chosen people considered that they were better than everyone else. When in reality they were just attempting to keep themselves unspotted from the ways of the world, and comply with the special requests that God had made of them as His covenant people. He said to them "For thou art an holy people unto the Lord thy God, and the Lord hath chosen thee to be a peculiar people unto himself" (Deuteronomy 14:2).

Isaiah likewise alludes to this special covenant relationship: "But thou Israel, art my servant, Jacob whom I have chosen, the seed of Abraham my friend" (Isaiah 41:8-9). In New Testament times he referred to the covenant line as "a royal priesthood, an holy nation, a peculiar people" (1 Peter 2:9). With this preferential status, how would a person who wanted to honor God be expected to act? Also, would it be very easy to offend someone who was not of "the Covenant?" To complicate matters, God not only required of Israel that they remain neutral from what the world was doing, but he added a responsibility upon their heads. They were to share the gospel message with the rest of the world, and extend an invitation to all who were willing to adhere to the strict code of conduct that being members of the covenant requires. All who were willing to enter into the covenant, and to commit to honoring the tenets of the faith that He had outlined as such, could be adopted into the House of Israel.

A person who is legally adopted takes on the name of the father who adopted them. They become legal heirs with those who were born into the family as blood heirs. This doctrine is spoken of frequently in the New Testament, particularly by the Apostle Paul. He doesn't deal with it secretly, but rather as a doctrine and practice that was a commonplace part of the good news of the gospel of Jesus Christ.

Two types of adoption are spoken of in the scriptures. A person who is of non-Israelite lineage becomes a member of the house of Israel through faith in Jesus Christ, when accompanied by baptism in water, and reception of the Holy Ghost, by the laying on of hands by those who are in authority to preach the gospel, and administer the ordinances thereof. The Savior himself alluded to this process when he answered the questions of Nicodemus (see John 3:5). In addition to this first type, all candidates for the fullness of salvation are counted as sons and daughters of Jesus Christ, being His children through adoption, on conditions of obedience to His gospel.

John the Baptist taught this concept though not actually using the term adoption in Matthew chapter three. When the Pharisees and Sadducees came to Him for baptism, He said to them: "And think not to say within yourselves, we have Abraham to our father: For I say unto you, that God is able of these stones to raise up children unto Abraham" (Matthew 3:7-9). As mentioned before, Paul taught of it on various occasions:

Who are Israelites; to whom pertaineth the adoption, and the glory, and the covenants, and the giving of the law, and the service of God, and the promises; . . . Not as though the word of God hath taken none effect. For they are not all Israel, which are of Israel (Romans 9:4,6).

In the eighth chapter of Romans he states that all who are truly adopted into the house of Israel become the children of Christ.

The Spirit itself beareth witness to our spirit, that we are the children of God: And if children, then heirs; heirs of God, and joint-heirs with Christ; if it so be that we suffer with him, that we may be also glorified together (see Romans 8:16-17).

He also taught the same doctrine to the Galatian saints (see Galatians 4), and to the Ephesians (see Ephesians 1:5).

Thus, it appears that the blessings of eternal life are available to all people regardless of race, creed, or color, who are willing to accept the true gospel of salvation, when it is offered to them by authorized members of Israel, and who are willing to be accepted into full fellowship, through baptism and the confirmation of the Holy Ghost at the hands of those duly authorized servants of the Lord. This point is illustrated in the eighth chapter of the book of Acts, where Peter, the acting president of the church, along with John, come to Samaria, when they hear that they have received the word of God.

> *Who, when they were come down, prayed for them, that they might receive the Holy Ghost:*
>
> *(For as yet he was fallen upon none of them: only they were baptized in the name of the Lord Jesus.)*
>
> *Then laid they their hands on them, and they received the Holy Ghost (Acts 8:15-17).*

We notice here that even though people had been baptized, they didn't automatically get the right to the Holy Ghost as a constant companion. It wasn't until the duly authorized servants of the Lord came, and actually confirmed them by the laying on of hands that they received the "gift of the Holy Ghost." A similar account follows in the nineteenth chapter, where Paul comes to Ephesus:

> *And finding certain disciples, he said unto them, have ye received the Holy Ghost since ye believed? And they said unto him, we have not so much as heard whether there be any Holy Ghost (Acts 19:1-2).*

After inquiring who baptized them it was evident that it was someone other than a duly authorized priesthood holder that had performed their baptisms. Then after instructing them in the true manner, he re-baptized them:

> *When they had heard this, they were baptized in the name of the Lord Jesus.*
>
> *And when Paul had laid his hands upon them, the Holy Ghost came upon them, and they spake with tongues and prophesied (Acts 19:5-6).*

Notice that the Holy Ghost isn't something that we can just assume to take for ourselves. It is a gift that must be bestowed upon us by a duly authorized servant of the Lord. Nonetheless it is evident that the influence of the Holy Ghost can be felt by virtually anyone on various occasions to help them in their conversion process as in Acts 2:37-41. After the people who were being taught the gospel were touched ("pricked") in their hearts, of the truthfulness of the message, Peter then informs them of how they could have the "gift of the Holy Ghost" bestowed upon them. It is also evident from this, and other passages, that there is a difference in feeling the influence of the Holy Ghost, and what is termed as the gift of the Holy Ghost.

These passages raise some puzzling questions: (1) Does it really matter who baptizes us? (2) What authority did Peter and Paul have that the other so-called ministers lacked, that would allow them to bestow the Holy Ghost on newly adopted members of the church? It's clear that only certain persons are authorized to act for the Savior in this adoption process. In Ephesians 4:4-5, Paul tells us that there is only one true baptism, and from these other passages it seems pretty clear that it is only valid when performed by the Lord's authorized servant.

19. *Say unto them, Thus saith the Lord God; Behold, I will take the stick of Joseph, which is in the hand of Ephraim, and the tribes of Israel his fellows, and will put them with him, even with the stick of Judah, and make them one stick, and they shall be one in mine hand.*

20. *And the sticks whereon thou writest shall be in thine hand before their eyes.*

21. *And say unto them, Thus saith the Lord God; Behold, I will take the children of Israel from among the heathen, whither they be gone, and will gather them on every side, and bring them into their own land:*

22. *And I will make them one nation in the land upon the mountains of Israel; and one king shall be king of them all: and they shall be no more two nations, neither shall they be divided into two kingdoms any more at all:*

—Ezekiel 37:19-22

CHAPTER 9
TWO RECORDS/ONE TRUE WAY

We've discussed the importance of the birthright in Israel, and how Joseph's posterity inherited it. We also learned that his posterity was carried away captive with the other tribes by Assyria. So what was to become of the Lord's promises to Joseph? He had been promised that his seed would receive a double portion both in the land of Canaan, and in another land choice above all others as their inheritance (see Genesis 48; 49:1, 22-26).

Because of the birthright, on him also would fall the responsibility of gathering the scattered of his brethren from throughout the earth. No other had the authority to do it because he was the birthright son. There are a number of allusions to this sacred responsibility throughout the Old Testament.

Ephraim is the one to whom it would ultimately fall, since he was the last link before the dispersion of the tribes. Joshua belonged to this tribe (Ephraim), and to him goes much of the credit for its subsequent greatness. Ephraim was a very jealous tribe by nature, and took exception to any successes attained by the other tribes. Their jealousy was a major reason for the division of the tribes into the north and south factions, discussed in chapter five.

It is to Isaiah that we look for the most in-depth information on the mission of Ephraim to reclaim (gather) scattered Israel in the last days. He begins chapter 11 with a prophecy of the coming of the Messiah. Christ was a descendant of King David, through his mother, Mary. David was the son of Jesse, and in the first two verses he tells of Christ (the stem) coming to earth then goes on and eludes to him as judging, surely speaking of his second coming, and continues by saying he shall smite the earth and slay the wicked (see Isaiah 11:4).

Then beginning in the tenth verse he begins a prophecy that we need to examine.

> And in that day there shall be a root of Jesse, which shall stand as an ensign (standard or banner) of the people; and to it shall the gentiles (non-Israelites) seek: and his rest shall be glorious.
>
> And it shall come to pass in that day, that the Lord shall set his hand again the second time to recover the remnant of his people, which shall be left, from Assyria, and from Egypt, and from Pathros, and from Cush, and from Elam, and from Shinar, and from Hamath, and from the islands of the sea.
>
> And he shall set up an ensign for the nations, and shall assemble the outcasts of Israel, and gather together the dispersed of Judah from the four corners of the earth. The envy of Ephraim shall depart, and the adversaries of Judah shall be cut off: Ephraim shall not envy Judah, and Judah shall not vex Ephraim (Isaiah 11:10-13).

He further speaks of the restoration of the gospel and the gathering of Israel in chapter 5:

> And he will lift up an ensign to the nations from far, and will hiss unto them from the end of the earth: and behold they shall come with speed swiftly (Isaiah 5:26).

So Israel is going to be gathered in the last days, and restored to the lands of their inheritance, and they will be one kingdom once again, with the tribe of Ephraim at the forefront. Christ will then reign on the earth, as their king, and there will be peace on the earth for a thousand years. This period is referred to as the Millennium. The question we need to answer is how is the Lord going to go about establishing all that?

The prophet Ezekiel tells us in the 37th chapter of his record. He was shown in vision how the Lord would bring this monumental event to pass:

> The word of the Lord came again unto me, saying,
>
> Moreover, thou son of man, take thee one stick and write upon it, For Judah, and for the children of Israel his companions: Then, take another stick, and write upon it, For Joseph, the stick of Ephraim, and for all the House of Israel, his companions:
>
> And join them one to another into one stick; and they shall become one in thine hand (Ezekiel 37:15-17).

A stick was a scroll or other object used to write upon. So Ezekiel is telling us that there was to be kept, the records of the house of Judah and the Lord's dealings with them, and also a record of the house of Joseph, through his birthright son Ephraim, and the Lord's dealings with them as well. And eventually the records of these two tribes, who were considered the chosen leaders of Israel by the Lord in former times, but who held a great amount of jealousy and animosity toward one another, would need to be joined together into one book. Or used together so to speak, in order to gather the blood of Israel from among the nations of the earth.

Let's continue on with his account:

> And when the children of thy people shall speak unto thee, saying, Wilt thou not show us what thou meanest by these?
>
> Say unto them, Thus saith the Lord God; Behold, I will take the stick of Joseph, which is in the hand of Ephraim, and the tribes of Israel his fellows, and will put them with him, even with the stick of Judah, and make them one stick, and they shall be one in mine hand.

And the sticks whereon thou writest shall be in thine hand before their eyes. And say unto them, Thus saith the Lord God; Behold I will take the children of Israel from among the heathen, whither they be gone, and will gather them on every side, and bring them into their own land:

And I will make them one nation in the land upon the mountains of Israel; And one king shall be king unto them all: And they shall be no more two nations, neither shall they be divided into two kingdoms any more at all:

Neither shall they defile themselves any more with their idols, nor with their detestable things, nor with any of their transgressions: but I will save them out of all their dwellingplaces, wherein they have sinned, and will cleanse them: so shall they be my people, and I will be their God.

And David my servant (referring to the stem of Jesse who is of the house of David or Jesus Christ) shall be king over them; and they all shall have one shepherd: they shall also walk in my judgments, and observe my statutes, and do them.

And they shall dwell in the land that I have given unto Jacob my servant, wherein your fathers have dwelt; and they shall dwell therein, even they, and their children, and their children's children for ever: and my servant David shall be their prince for ever.

Moreover I will make a covenant of peace with them; it shall be an everlasting covenant with them: and I will place them, and multiply them, and will set my sanctuary in the midst of them forever more.

My tabernacle (temple) also shall be with them: yea, I will be their God, and they shall be my people.

And the heathen shall know that I the Lord do sanctify Israel, when my sanctuary shall be in the midst of them forever more (Ezekiel 37:18-28).

I submit that the information, which Ezekiel shares with us in these verses, is some of the most valuable insights in all of holy writ. With precision he reveals to us the plan of our Father in Heaven, for his chosen house in the last days, when he will destroy all evil from off the earth, and re-establish His kingdom once again upon the earth. Then He will send His Son the second time to redeem them from their lost and fallen state. It seems to be very clear in his words that the writings of both Judah and Joseph are going to be required to accomplish this monumental task. And with what we have learned of the birthright and its importance, I wonder which of the two records would be the most vital to that mission?

When I have posed this question to serious seekers of the truth over the years, they have invariably said, "The record of Joseph, because he is the one with the authority to lead in Israel." To which I wholeheartedly agree. There seems to be one major problem . . . where is it?! We know that the record of the Bible . . . the record of the house of Judah, or the Jews, is truly the word of God, but nowhere have I ever found anyone who has a clue as to the whereabouts of the "most vital record," the record of the people of Joseph, the birthright tribe.

We, as Christians, all know the Bible to be the word of God, but from the mouths of god-fearing people themselves, there appears to be a missing piece of the scriptural puzzle, which is as important, or actually of more importance to the salvation of man, than the Bible. Some may look at that kind of a statement as blasphemous or pagan. But I don't believe it is, as I'm sure you can now see, when taken in the context of the information we have just uncovered.

There appear to be a number of missing records according to the Bible itself: the book of the wars of the Lord (see Numbers 21:14); book of Jashar (see Joshua 10:13; 2 Samuel 1:18); the Acts of Solomon (see 1 Kings 11:41); Samuel the Seer, Gad the Seer, and Nathan the prophet (see I Chronicles 29:29); prophecy of Ahijah (see 2 Chronicles 9:29); the visions of Iddo the seer, (see 2 Chronicles 9:29; 12:15; 13:22); book of Shemaiah (see 2 Chronicles 12:15); book of Jehu (see 2 Chronicles 2:34); sayings of the Seers (see 2 Chronicles 33:19); an epistle from Paul to the Corinthians, earlier than our present book of 1st Corinthians (see 1 Corinthians 5:9); possibly an earlier epistle to the Ephesians (see Ephesians 3:3); an epistle to the church at Laodicea (see Colossians 4:16); and some prophecies of Enoch, known to Jude (see Jude 1:14); the book of the covenant (see Exodus 24:7), which may or may not be included in the present Book of Exodus; the manner of the kingdom (see 1 Samuel 10:25) written by Samuel; and the rest of the acts of Uzziah written by Isaiah (see 2 Chronicles 26:22), to name a few. We can apparently get along without the books just listed, but a book of the obvious importance of the book of Joseph is absolutely imperative, as Ezekiel points out. Why? Well, quite simply put, that's the way God wants it. Ours is not to question, but to obey. It appears to all go back to the covenant that he made with Abraham as mentioned in chapter one. There are certain covenants that each of us must enter into and keep if we would have eternal life with Him and live again in His presence.

The Bible is replete with evidences of this fact: when the Lord delivered Israel the first time he used Moses as an instrument in His hands to bring them out of Egypt. He then led them to Mount Sinai to give them His higher law, and the covenants that pertained thereto. But because of their rebellious nature, He withdrew his offer, and instead gave them a lesser law, the law of Moses, which told them basically every step to take, and every thing to do.

The casual reader of the scriptures will remember that Moses threw down the tablets, which contained the Ten Commandments when he came down from the mountain and discovered that the children of Israel had made a golden calf and were involved in the worship of it, as well as in immoral behavior. But if you read the account more closely, you will discover a little different version of the story. We'll start in the 19th chapter of Exodus, where Moses climbs Sinai to converse with the Lord:

> *And Moses went up unto God, and the Lord called unto him out of the mountain, saying, Thus shalt thou say to the house of Jacob, and tell the children of Israel;*
>
> *Ye have seen what I did to the Egyptians, and how I bare you on eagles wings, and brought you unto myself.*

Now therefore, if you will obey my voice indeed, and keep my covenant, then ye shall be a peculiar treasure unto me above all people: for all the earth is mine:

And ye shall be unto me a kingdom of priests, and an holy nation. These are the words, which thou shalt speak unto the children of Israel (Exodus 19:3-6).

He also gives to them the Ten Commandments and Moses returns to the camp and delivers the message. The people answer "All that the Lord hath spoken we will do." So he returns again to report to the Lord, whereupon the Lord sends him back with the instructions to sanctify themselves, and prepare themselves to go up to the mountain of the Lord, to enter into this sacred covenant he had established with their father, Abraham. He returns and puts them under covenant, instructing them in various things that would be expected of them as His covenant people.

The Lord instructed the children of Israel to build a temple in which to worship Him. But since they were going to be a bit transient for a while they were instructed to make it portable. It would be called the tabernacle.

Meanwhile, Moses returns to the mountain to commune with the Lord. This time he is gone for forty days, and when the people see that he hasn't returned they think he's not coming back and they pressure Aaron into making them a golden calf to worship. Because of the Lord's displeasure, He caused them to stay in the wilderness until all of the generation that had rebelled had passed on. And because he saw that they were as little children in their spiritual maturity he gave them the lesser law, which was administered by the priesthood of Aaron. This lesser law was to prepare them to someday be able to live the higher law that Jesus would bring in the future, when He would be born to Mary and Joseph into mortality. This lesser set of laws was intended to be a schoolmaster, to prepare them, and help them prepare to accept the higher law He would bring at that future time (see Galatians 3:19-29).

What does all of this rambling have to do with the missing book of Joseph? Well, going back to the covenant made with

Joseph, that his seed would get a double portion of land, both in the promised land of Canaan, and in another over the water, and choice above all others. God doesn't break His promises, so how, with the tribes of Ephraim and Manasseh lost with the other eight tribes in the north countries, was the promise to be fulfilled? In the next chapter we'll find out.

22. Joseph is a fruitful bough, even a fruitful bough by a well;
whose branches run over the wall:

—Genesis 49:22

CHAPTER 10
A PROMISE HONORED

As was discussed in chapters six and seven, various prophets were sent to testify to Israel and to Judah of their wickedness, and warn them to repent or suffer the consequences. In addition to Isaiah, Jeremiah, and Ezekiel, mentioned in the stick of Judah (the Bible), there were others. One of these not mentioned was a prophet named Lehi, who was a descendant of the loins of Joseph, and a resident of Jerusalem around the year 600 B.C. Like the others, he faced persecution, and public outrage from the rebellious Jews in the city. They hurled insults at him, and threatened him with bodily harm if he didn't cease his teachings against them. As he was laboring under these turbulent conditions, he was praying one night for the welfare of the city, when his mind was caught away in a vision. He saw the city of Jerusalem, that it would be destroyed, and that many of its inhabitants would either be slain or carried away captive into Babylon. Because of the things, which he saw and heard, he continued to preach to them with the hope that they might be moved to repentance. But alas, they would not, and instead they mocked him because of the many things of which he testified against them. For he bore down in pure testimony against them of their wickedness and abominations, and they were angry. During these trying times the Lord spoke to Lehi in a dream, and comforted him, telling him that he had done what he had been called to do, and that He had accepted his service in Jerusalem. He also told him that because the people sought his life, and their hearts were sufficiently hardened that they would not repent, their time of destruction was growing near. He told Lehi to take his family and depart into the wilderness so he and his family would not be a part of that impending destruction. Being a man of obedience to the requests of the Lord, he did as he was commanded. He and his wife Sariah took their family, and packed up what little they could take, then departed into the wilderness.

God continued to communicate with this prophet, guiding him in their travels. The little group spent the better part of eight years wandering in the wilderness, being led, protected, and supported by God. As mentioned earlier, this was the same time period in which Nebuchadnezzar swooped down upon Jerusalem and validated the prophecies of Lehi and the other prophets. Somewhere around 592 B.C., after traveling a distance that some have calculated to be as much as over 2,100 miles from Jerusalem, they came to a large body of water. The Lord then instructed them in how to construct a ship, which they would use to cross over the waters. They sailed the great deep, being guided by God, through a peculiar compass that worked according to their faith, and being driven forth upon the water by the winds God provided, they finally landed somewhere in the Americas.

Great story you might say, but what does it have to do with anything we've been talking about here? That's a good question. We learned earlier that the Lord had promised that a remnant of Joseph's seed would be spared, and receive an inheritance in a promised land, choice above all others, that he was a fruitful bough by a well (water), and that "his branches" (posterity) would "run over the wall" (see Genesis 49:22).

According to their genealogy, Lehi's family had a very interesting lineage. Even though they lived in Jerusalem, they weren't of the house of Judah. As they were sojourning in the wilderness Lehi began to read the writings of the records they took with them, and we are given some very enlightening information:

> Lehi, took the records which were engraven on the plates of brass, and he did search them from the beginning.

And he beheld that they did contain the five books of Moses, which gave an account of the creation of the world, and also of Adam and Eve, who were our first parents;

And also a record of the Jews from the beginning, even down to the commencement of the reign of Zedekiah, king of Judah;

And also many prophecies which have been spoken by the mouth of Jeremiah.

And it came to pass that . . . Lehi, also found upon the plates of brass a genealogy of his fathers; wherefore he knew that he was a descendant of Joseph, yea, even that Joseph who was the son of Jacob, who was sold into Egypt, and who was preserved . . . that he might preserve his father, Jacob, and all his household from perishing with famine.

And they were also led out of captivity, and out of the land of Egypt, by that same God who had preserved them (1Nephi 5:10-15).

Well, there you have it, the welding link between the stick of Judah (the Bible), and the prophesied stick of Joseph. The piece that has been missing to the grand puzzle that is the house of Israel, has at last been found, and has been joined together with its companion the Holy Bible. It is a record, which divinely claims to be the missing stick, or book, of the house of Joseph. Its teachings were recorded on thin plates of gold, and give the accounts of the Lord's dealings with this chosen line of His covenant people.

The record was written by His holy prophets whom He called to minister to His children in the Americas, just as he did in Jerusalem. I will quote from the words of Nephi, the son of Lehi, another prophet who wrote in the sacred writings of the loins of Joseph, to further illustrate my point:

And now I, Nephi, do not give the genealogy of my fathers in this part of my record; neither at any time shall I give it after upon these plates which I am writing; for it is given in the record which has been kept by my father; wherefore, I do not write it in this work.

For it sufficeth me to say that we are descendants of Joseph (1 Nephi 6:1-2).

He then goes on to state the purpose of this sacred, second record:

For the fullness of mine intent is that I may persuade men to come unto the God of Abraham, and the God of Isaac, and the God of Jacob, and be saved (1 Nephi 6:4).

The record continues, covering the period of time from 600 B.C. to approximately 421 A.D. The crowning event in this book is when the Savior personally visits the ancient people on the American continent, shortly after His resurrection, telling them that they are the ones He spoke of in the book of John:

And other sheep I have which are not of this fold: them also I must bring, and they shall hear my voice; and there shall be one fold, and one shepherd (John 10:14-16).

The record is an abridgement of the records of the house of Joseph as kept by the Lord's prophets on the American continent. It was abridged by a prophet whose name was Mormon. Mormon's son Moroni was the last prophet to write in the record. He finished the record, and buried it in a stone box, on the side of a hill in what today is upstate New York. He would return some 1,400 years later to that same hillside, and deliver it to a young man who was a descendant of both ephraim and Judah. This man would then be called to be the prophet of the restoration. His name was Joseph Smith, and it was he who would in turn bring it and its teachings to light in the last days. It was to be joined together with the Bible, in order to gather scattered Israel.

The stick of Joseph when translated would be given the name of the prophet who abridged it. It is known today as the Book of Mormon, and is a second witness of Jesus Christ and his divinity. The prophet Isaiah prophesied of such a record:

For the Lord hath poured out upon you the spirit of deep sleep, and hath closed your eyes: the prophets and your rulers, the seers hath he covered.

And the vision of all is become unto you as the words of a book that is sealed, which men deliver to one that is learned, saying, Read this I pray thee: and he saith, I cannot; for it is sealed:

And the book is delivered to him that is not learned, saying, Read this, I pray thee: and he saith, I am not learned.

Wherefore the Lord said, Forasmuch as this people draw near me with their mouth, and with their lips do honor me, but have removed their heart far from me, and their fear toward me is taught by the precept of men:

Therefore, behold, I will proceed to do a marvellous work among this people, even a marvellous work and a wonder: for the wisdom of their wise men shall perish, and the under-standing of their prudent men shall be hid . . .

Therefore thus saith the Lord, who redeemed Abraham, concerning the house of Jacob, Jacob shall not now be ashamed, neither shall his face now wax pale.

But when he seeth his children, the work of mine hands, in the midst of him, they shall sanctify my name, and sanctify the name of the Holy One of Jacob . . .

They also that erred in spirit shall come to understanding, and they that murmured shall learn doctrine (Isaiah 29:10-14, 22-24).

Thus, in a few simple, straightforward statements we each have a very poignant dilemma placed before us. As I see it, we must each choose either to ignore the claims that these ancient prophets made, that indeed there is another book divinely written to be the second vital witness (see Matthew 18:6; 2 Corinthians 13:1), that Jesus Christ is the son of the living God and the Savior of the world, and our advocate with the Father. Or with a humble heart, and an open mind, we can read this record in the light of what it claims to be. I have yet to meet anyone who has even so much as heard of this record, let alone claim to know of its whereabouts. A record that prophets of God have testified to the world must come forth to be joined with the Bible to establish truth, and gather the house of Israel in the last days. Reason alone should tell us that we ought to at least read it before we judge it to be untrue, unless we already claim to have found this missing record elsewhere. Otherwise, it would seem rather foolish and shortsighted to dismiss the Book of Mormon's credibility without considering its contents.

26. But the Comforter, which is the Holy Ghost, whom the Father will send in my name, he shall teach you all things, and bring all things to your remembrance, whatsoever I have said unto you.

—John 14:26

CHAPTER 11

THE MISSION OF THE HOLY GHOST

One of the defining doctrines of the Church of Jesus Christ of Latter-day Saints is its concept of the Godhead. Many in the Christian world believe that Latter-day Saints worship a different God and Christ than they do. This chapter has a twofold purpose. It is an attempt to (1) teach the tenets; and (2) explain from the scriptures the basis for these tenets.

The Holy Ghost is the third member of the Godhead, and differs from our Heavenly Father and Jesus Christ in that it is a personage of spirit, rather than a possessor of a resurrected body of flesh and bones. In order to understand this doctrine, let us begin by going to the beginning of the Bible, in the book of Genesis. As stated in chapter seven, God knew us before we were formed in the womb (see Jeremiah 1:5). Latter-day Saints believe that before each of us was born into mortality we lived in a premortal existence. There, our Heavenly Father created our spirits, and as stated in Genesis chapter 1, part of our eternal progression was for each of us to come to earth, and gain a mortal experience:

> *And God said, Let us make man in our image, after our like-ness. So God created man in his own image, in the image of God created he him; male and female created he them (Genesis 1:26-28).*

Latter-day Saints take God at His word. They believe that things are just as they read in this passage. In His own image and likeness mean exactly that. What are we like? We are immortal spirits housed in mortal physical bodies, which were created by God in His own image, and after His own likeness. You will also notice in the previous scripture, that the wording is "let us." Obviously our Father in Heaven wasn't acting alone in this creation process. Latter-day Saints believe that the pre-mortal Jehovah, or Jesus, was right there alongside the Father in the creation. In fact we believe that as is stated in the first chapter of the book of John, Christ was given the assignment of carrying out the work of the creation of the earth (see John 1:1-15). Latter-day Saints feel that the Father and the Son are separate and distinct individuals, and that they both have glorified bodies of flesh and bone, tangible as man's, but perfected and immortal, unlike man's at this stage of his existence. However, they believe that the Holy Ghost is a personage of spirit, making it so he can not dwell within us.

The Holy Ghost has been manifest in every dispensation of the gospel since the time Adam and Eve left the Garden of Eden. And as stated before, it is manifested to men and women on the earth, both as the power of the Holy Ghost, and the gift of the Holy Ghost. The power can be manifested to a person before baptism, and is to be the convincing witness that the gospel is true (see John 14:26; 15; 26). It instills in a person the testimony of Jesus Christ and of His work, and of His work through His servants here on the earth. The gift of the Holy Ghost is the right to have its companionship and influence with us, and is only possible according to our individual worthiness. The gift can only come after proper and authorized baptism, and is conferred only by the laying on of hands. More powerful than that which we experience before baptism, it acts as a cleansing agent to purify a person and sanctify him/her from all sin. Thus it is often spoken of as "fire" (see Matthew 3:11). The manifestations at the day of Pentecost were the gift of the Holy Ghost, which came upon the twelve, without which they would not have been ready for their ministries to the world (see Acts 2).

For some unexplained reason the Holy Ghost didn't operate in its fullness among the Jews during the years of the Savior's mortal ministry (see John 7:39; 16:7-8). Statements to this effect, that it wouldn't come until after the resurrection of the Savior, would have to be referring to that dispensation only, because it is evident that the Holy Ghost was abundantly operative in Old Testament times. And furthermore they would, of necessity, be referring to the gift of the Holy Ghost not being present, since the power of the Holy Ghost was operative during the ministry of John the Baptist, and the Savior himself. If that were not the case, none would have been able to receive a true testimony of the gospel that Jesus Christ taught (see Matthew 16:16-17; I Corinthians 12:3). When a person speaks, he speaks words. But when someone speaks by the power of the Holy Ghost, it carries a conviction to the spirit of the listeners. It is only then that a true testimony is born. It is then that it carries a true conviction to the heart of any true seeker of truth. The Holy Ghost knows all things, and can even lead one to know of future events (see 2 Peter 1:21).

The Holy Ghost is also referred to by other titles in the scriptures such as; Holy Spirit, Comforter, Spirit of God, Spirit of the Lord, and simply as the Spirit. People have often asked me to prove to them that what we teach or believe is true, or to explain to them how I know it is true. My answer to that question is quite simple. Nobody can give someone else a testimony of anything. There are many times we would like to be able to give someone that burning conviction of the truthfulness of what we believe or know to be true. But the truth is, that a true testimony can only come through the witness of the Holy Ghost to the spirit of humble people, who seek it from above. It is the power by which we can all receive our own personal revelation, not from any man, but from our Father Himself. If what we have is true, the Holy Ghost will reveal it to anyone who sincerely seeks to know of its truthfulness (see James 1:4-5).

To conclude this chapter, I quote the prophet Moroni's testimony to the world, as he closed his writing in the Book of Mormon, concerning the mission of the Holy Ghost in the pursuit of truth and light.

And I seal up these records, after I have spoken a few words by way of exhortation unto you.

Behold, I would exhort you that when ye shall read these things, if it be wisdom in God that ye should read them, that ye would remember how merciful the Lord hath been unto the children of men, from the creation of Adam even down until the time ye shall receive these things, and ponder it in your hearts.

And when ye shall receive these things, I would exhort you that ye would ask God, the Eternal Father, in the name of Christ, if these things are not true; and if ye shall ask with a sincere heart, with real intent, having faith in Christ, he will manifest the truth of it unto you, by the power of the Holy Ghost.

And by the Power of the Holy Ghost ye may know the truth of all things (Moroni 10:2-5).

4. *And no man taketh this honour unto himself, but he that is called of God, as was Aaron.*

—Hebrews 5:4

CHAPTER 12

PRIESTHOOD AUTHORITY, WHO HAS IT?

When the Savior came to John the Baptist to receive baptism, John was baptizing people in the River Jordan. Why did the Savior come to him to be baptized, and not just anybody? The answer is given by John himself, in telling the Pharisees and Sadducees:

> *I indeed baptize you with water unto repentance: but he that cometh after me is mightier than I, whose shoes I am not worthy to bear: he shall baptize you with the Holy Ghost, and with fire" (Matthew 3:11).*

What did he mean by that? What was he really saying? John was from the lineage of Levi, and therefore had the right to hold the Priesthood of Aaron, or Levitical Priesthood.

After Israel had rebelled under the leadership of Moses, they had the right to a higher priesthood taken from them. All of the ancient prophets would have needed to hold it, but the right to hold it was basically taken from the common man. Only males of the tribe of Levi were allowed to hold the priesthood, and then, only the lesser priesthood at that. The Aaronic Priesthood carries the authority to perform only the outward ordinances of the gospel, such as baptism, and John, in the preceding state-ment manifests that such is the case. That is why, in Matthew chapter eight that fact was illustrated in citing the two examples, of Peter, and of Paul, conferring the gift of the Holy Ghost. John didn't hold the higher priesthood, but the Savior did, and he would later confer it on the heads of His apostles before His mortal mission was over, so they could carry on the work he had started. Speaking to Peter, the Lord said:

> *I will give unto thee the keys of the kingdom of heaven: and whatsoever thou shalt bind on earth shall be bound in heaven: And whatsoever thou shalt loose on earth shall be loosed in heaven (Matthew 16:19).*

Those priesthood keys he was referring to included the power for men on earth to perform acts that would be binding beyond this life. The fact that there is a higher priesthood, and that the Savior, Himself, held it is made manifest in the writings of Paul to the Hebrews. Paul speaks of this priesthood authority in a few places, but I will cite only Hebrews chapters five and seven. He states:

> *And no man taketh this honor unto himself, but he that is called of God, as was Aaron.*

> *So also Christ glorified not himself to be made an high priest; but he that said unto him, Thou art my Son, to day have I begotten thee. As he saith also in another place, Thou art a priest for ever after the order of Melchisedec (Hebrews 5:5-6).*

We see that Christ, Himself, was given the higher or Melchizedek Priesthood, by Heavenly Father, and there are strict instructions to us that we cannot just assume to take God's holy priesthood to ourselves. We must have it conferred on us by someone who already has it to bestow, and only after we are adopted into the house of Israel through baptism.

If this sounds like a strange and new doctrine . . . it's not. Why, even Simon the sorcerer testified of it. Let's refer back to the story cited earlier in the book of Acts, when Peter and John were conferring the Holy Ghost on the newly baptized members in Samaria:

> *But there was a certain man called Simon, which beforetime in the same city used sorcery, and bewitched the people of Samaria, giving out that he himself was some great one.*

> *To whom they all gave heed, from the least to the greatest, saying This man is the great power of God.*

> *And to him they had regard, because of the long time he had bewitched them with sorceries (Acts 8:9-11).*

Here was a man who clearly used the power of the underworld to his advantage. But when he heard the preaching of Philip, even he believed, and was baptized. "And when he was baptized, he continued with Philip, and wondered, beholding the miracles and signs which were done" (Acts 8:13). Then after he witnessed the conferral of the Holy Ghost by the laying on of hands, under the authority of this higher priesthood, he recognized that it was far superior to the power of Satan that he had heretofore used.

We'll pick up the story in verse 18:

> And when Simon saw that through the laying on of the Apostle's hands, the Holy Ghost was given, he offered them money,
>
> Saying give me also this power, that whomsoever I lay hands, he may receive the Holy Ghost.
>
> But Peter said unto him, Thy money perish with thee, because thou hast thought that the gift of God may be purchased with money (Acts 8:18-20).

The Lord personally took a hard line against those who took it upon themselves to be his representatives, without going through the proper channels. He said:

> Not every one that saith unto me, Lord, Lord, shall enter into the kingdom of heaven; but he that doeth the will of my father which is in heaven.
>
> Many will say to me in that day, Lord, Lord, have we not prophesied in thy name? and in thy name have cast out devils? and in thy name done many wonderful works?
>
> And then I will profess unto them, I never knew you: depart from me, ye that work iniquity (Matthew 7:21-23).

On the surface, that may seem like a rather sharp rebuke to individuals who were sincerely trying to do the right thing. But let's pursue it a little. Let's say that you have sympathies for those persons who want so badly to enter the United States from another country. You feel that they are being wronged, and it is beginning to become an obsession with you to see to it that all can have the chance of the better life that those who are U.S.

citizens have. You hear of some horrible tragedies where many have died from exposure, because they felt they had to sneak over U.S. borders to succeed. You finally take it upon yourself to go to the border to take matters into your own hands. You may have even managed to get yourself a uniform and a badge so that you would look official. Now, let's say that you encounter some of those who are coming into the country without going through the proper process, and you tell them that you are an official immigration officer, with the authority to allow them to enter the country. And let's say that because of your uniform and your convincing words, that they believe you. In fact, let's say that you have become so zealous in your crusade that you have actually come to believe that you are authorized yourself.

If they enter the country and truly authorized officers apprehend them, what will happen to them? Do you think that the officers will listen to their story and allow them to stay? Of course not! Whether they should have more freedom isn't the issue here, it is the fact that you don't have the authority to act in the name of the government. Apparently God feels the same way about those who assume the authority to perform the saving ordinances of His gospel, in His name, without His official sanction. And just like the illegal immigrants, who will be deported, so likewise will many, who think they have had those ordinances performed, be denied entrance into His kingdom, unless they are eventually performed by the proper priesthood authority.

Now, back to Hebrews where we began this chapter on priesthood authority. We were discussing the fact that the Savior held the Melchisedec (Melchizedek) priesthood. In Hebrews 5:9-10 it reads: "And being made perfect, he became the author of eternal salvation unto all them that obey him; Called of God an high priest after the order of Melchisedec." Hebrews seven gives us more information on this higher priesthood:

For this Melchisedec, king of Salem, priest of the most high God, who met Abraham returning from the slaughter of the kings, and blessed him;

To whom also Abraham gave a tenth part of all; first being by interpretation King of righteousness, and after that King of Salem, which is King of peace;

Without father, without mother, without descent, having neither beginning of days, nor end of life; but made like unto the Son of God; abideth a priest continually (Hebrews 7:1-3).

Now consider how great this man was, unto whom even the patriarch Abraham gave the tenth of the spoils.

And verily they that are of the sons of Levi, who receive the office of the priesthood, have a commandment to take tithes of the people according to the law, that is, of their brethren, though they come out of the loins of Abraham (Hebrews 7:5).

When the Melchizedek Priesthood was taken from Israel, and they were put under the administration of the Aaronic Priesthood, and given the law of Moses to live by, this was to prepare them for when the Messiah would come and reinstate the ordinances of the Melchizedek Priesthood. This has led to a great deal of confusion throughout the annals of time, which we will discuss in chapter 16.

Perfection doesn't come through the ordinances of the lesser priesthood, but only through those of the higher law. If the people could learn to live by lesser commandments, then hopefully they would be able to one day live the more stringent ones that the Savior would bring at His first coming:

If therefore perfection were by the Levitical priesthood, (for under it the people received the law,) what further need was there that another priest should rise after the order of Melchisedec, and not be called after the order of Aaron?

For the priesthood being changed, there is made of necessity a change also of the law" (Hebrews 7:11-12).

It was through the power and authority of this higher priesthood that Jesus, and His apostles after Him, raised the dead, gave the blind their sight, made the lame to walk, the deaf to hear, and the dumb to speak, cast out devils from those who were possessed, how Moses parted the Red Sea, and how the Master had power over the sea, and all the elements. The priesthood of God is literally the power of God, given to man, to act in his name, and have it recognized by Him.

It is the witness of the Church of Jesus Christ of Latter-day Saints that the very priesthood, which Christ and His ancient apostles held, is given to man on the earth today. People can say what they may, but I have been a witness to its healing power on many occasions. I have lived to see the sick and afflicted be made whole in a miraculous manner, and to literally see people raised from their deathbeds, through priesthood administrations. If what we are saying is true, and I testify that it is, it is of the utmost significance to all of mankind. The question I would pose is this: What blessings would be added to the lives of people, who don't now know of it, if they were to have access to that priesthood power?

15. *And account that the longsuffering of our Lord is salvation;*
    even as our beloved brother Paul also according to the
    wisdom given unto him hath written unto you;
16. *As also in all his epistles, speaking in them of these things; in*
    which are somethings hard to be understood, which they that
    are unlearned and unstable wrest, as they do also the other
    scriptures, unto their own destruction.

—2 Peter 3:15-16

CHAPTER 13
A BIBLE! A BIBLE!

But behold, there shall be many—at that day when I shall proceed to do a marvelous work among them, that I may remember my covenants which I have made to the children of men, that I may set my hand again the second time to recover my people, which are of the house of Israel;

And also, that I may remember the promises which I have made unto thee, Nephi, and also unto thy father, that I would remember your seed; and that the words of your seed should proceed forth out of my mouth unto your seed; and my words shall hiss forth unto the ends of the earth, for a standard unto my people, which are of the house of Israel;

And because my words shall hiss forth—many of the gentiles shall say: A Bible! A Bible! We have got a Bible, and there cannot be any more Bible.

But thus saith the Lord God: O fools, they shall have a Bible: and it shall proceed forth from the Jews, mine ancient covenant people. And what thank they the Jews for the Bible which they receive from them? Yea, what do the Gentiles mean? Do they remember the travails, and the labors, and the pains of the Jews, and their diligence unto me, in bringing forth salvation unto the Gentiles?

O ye gentiles, have ye remembered the Jews, mine ancient covenant people? Nay; but ye have cursed them, and have hated them, and have not sought to recover them. But behold

I will return all these things upon your own heads; for I the Lord have not forgotten my people.

Thou fool, that shall say: A Bible, we have got a Bible, and we need no more Bible. Have ye obtained a Bible save it were by the Jews? Know ye not that there are more nations than one.

Know ye not that I, the Lord your God, have created all men, and that I remember those who are upon the isles of the sea; and that I rule in the heavens above and in the earth beneath; and I bring forth my word unto the children of men, yea, even upon all the nations of the earth?

Wherefore murmur ye, because that ye shall receive more of my word? Know ye not that the testimony of two nations is a witness unto you that I am God, that I remember one nation like unto another? Wherefore, I speak the same words unto one nation like unto another. And when the two nations shall run together the testimony of the two nations shall run together also.

And I do this that I may prove unto many that I am the same yesterday, today, and forever; and that I speak forth my words according to mine own pleasure. And because that I have spoken one word ye need not suppose that I cannot speak another; for my work is not yet finished; neither shall it be until the end of man, neither from that time henceforth and forever.

Wherefore, because that ye have a Bible ye need not suppose that it contains all my words; neither need ye suppose that I have not caused more to be written.

For I command all men, both in the east and in the west, and in the north, and in the south, and in the islands of the sea, that they shall write the words that I speak unto them; for out of the books which shall be written I will judge the world, every man according to their works, according to that which is written (2 Nephi 29:1-11).

That is the way one chapter of the Book of Mormon begins. Isn't it ironic that the Christian world looks at the Jewish nation with such contempt because they don't believe that Jesus Christ was divine and thus, not the Promised Messiah. Yet these same people hinge all of their religious faith on, and derive all their doctrinal dogma from the Old and New Testament, which is the stick of Judah, or record of the Jews?! When we look at it in that light, it doesn't make a whole lot of sense, does it? If we are not careful, we will become so closed-minded that we can shut ourselves off from our learning the truth, when it comes our way.

In college, while I was doing my undergraduate work, I had the experience of taking a class on social psychology. The professor was your typical stereotype teacher of psychology. He wore deerskin shoes, and a suede leather jacket, and smoked a pipe. He was balding on top, and had graying hair around his temples, and a large, bushy white mustache. On one of the first days of class, he posed an interesting question to us. He asked, "What is truth?"

I answered with a quote from the scriptures, though I didn't mention that in my answer. I said, "Truth is knowledge of things as they are, as they were, and as they are to come."

He bluntly stated, "Incorrect!"

A bit taken back, I replied, "What do you mean?"

He then gave his own version, which supposedly was the "true" definition. He said, "Truth is whatever the individual perceives it to be."

Feeling a bit bewildered, I prodded him to elaborate a bit on just what it was that he was saying. He then went to great lengths to have us understand that everyone can have their own truth based on how they see things. Feeling duty bound, having recently returned from serving a two-year church mission, to try and undo the false premises that he was teaching the rest of the class, I pulled out a silver (at least that's what color it appeared to be) pen and proceeded to ask him what color it was. His answer? You guessed it! It was whatever color I perceived it to be. I believe he was actually serious about his definition of truth. But it also seemed to me that his approach to truth would give him a very convenient alibi, should he do things that might be deemed by others as wrong.

I decided to give it one more attempt, and I asked him, "So if I perceived you to be a menace to society, if that were my truth, would it be okay if I killed you? Would that be acceptable?" As I remember, he didn't really have an answer for me, but looked at me as though to ask, "How did I ever get you in my class?"

I've thought about his definition a lot over the years since. Things are as they are . . . period! It doesn't really change the way they really are, just because you or I may not want to accept, or deal with it. Truth doesn't disappear, or cease to be, just because you or I may not like it. To think like that would be ludicrous.

Our Heavenly Father deals with us according to eternal principles, and He would cease to be God, if He were to act contrary to them. He doesn't lower His standards for us, so that we can qualify for salvation, and still return to Him after we lived our own individual truths. No, to the contrary. He gives us eternal gospel truths, and then asks us to raise our standards to their level. In a sense, that is what many in the Christian world seem to have done with the scriptures. There are literally thousands of different Christian religions (churches) on the earth today. None of them is exactly identical to another, and they differ and contradict each other on various points of doctrine. That is why the Book of Mormon is such a vital resource. If it is truly the missing stick of Joseph, the doctrines Christ taught while filling his mortal ministry cannot be twisted or misinterpreted by man's personal interpretations or biases. Its writings will clarify those doctrines so that there can truly be a unity of the faith throughout Christianity.

Let's take the church Christ established as our silver pen. Every person out there could have their own private interpretation of, what this scripture meant, or what that doctrine was, etc., but if we are truly interested in finding truth, it doesn't really matter what "we" think. What really matters is what the Savior says. Who are we that we should decide truth? The Bible is not open to private interpretation by us as individuals. So why is Biblical meaning so confusing to the Christian world in general? Let's examine it and see.

Suppose someone that was not affiliated with the Church of Jesus Christ of Latter-day Saints and knew nothing of its teachings, were to overhear two people talking about going to a dance at the stake center that night, or that they were going to go the one of the temples to receive their endowments? What would they assume to be happening in each of these situations? In the first case, they would probably be disappointed when they got to the dance and discovered that the dance was at the *stake,* not *steak,* center. A stake is comprised of a group of wards, or congregations, encompassing a specific geographical area. Therefore a stake center is a church building. An endowment today is generally recognized as a gift of money, donated to an organization or cause. The term *endowment* in the Church refers to an endowment of power, through covenants made with God, and it is one of the higher ordinances connected with the Melchizedek Priesthood, and they are only performed in sacred temples. We might well see by now, that unless a person has a basic understanding of the Abrahamic covenant, and subsequently, the birthright, and the history of the House of Israel past, present, and future, he/she won't be able to understand the meanings of many of the teachings in the Old Testament. Likewise there are similar overtones in the New Testament: Let's closely examine the writings of the apostle Paul, who wrote over half of the New Testament, and from whose writings the world's Christian religions get a good portion of their doctrinal information. We must first understand whom he was writing to, and about the circumstances that led to the epistles he wrote.

Paul was an avid missionary, whose zeal to share the truth was unprecedented, that is except for the Savior Himself. He made three major missionary journeys during his ministry, teaching and baptizing converts, and establishing branches of the church along the way. His letters to those various branches of the church are where we get much of Christianity's doctrinal dogma. Peter, the presiding head over Christ's church after the crucifixion of the Savior, wrote to future New Testament readers speaking of events in the latter-days, and signs of the second coming:

> *Wherefore, beloved, seeing that ye look for such things, be diligent that ye may be found of him in peace, without spot, and blameless.*

And account that the long-suffering of our Lord is salvation; even as our beloved brother Paul also according to the wisdom given unto him hath written unto you;

As also in all his epistles, speaking in them of these things; in which are some things hard to be understood, which they that are unlearned, and unstable wrest (twist or distort), as they do also other scriptures, unto their own destruction.

Ye therefore, beloved, seeing ye know these things before, beware lest ye also, being led away with the error of the wicked, fall from your own steadfastness (2 Peter 3:14-17).

That appears to me to be a warning of epic proportions, and one that we all would do well to understand and heed. According to Peter, Paul's writings are going to be misunderstood, and misinterpreted by many, and it just may cost them their salvation. Why? For an answer to that question, let me cite a few scriptures that hopefully will help illustrate why so many churches, with so many conflicting points of doctrine, exist. Paul begins his letters by introducing himself, and telling who each particular letter was written to:

Paul, a servant of Jesus Christ, called to be an apostle, separated unto the gospel of God . . . Among whom are ye also the called of Jesus Christ:

To all that be in Rome, beloved of God, called to be saints (Romans 1:1, 6-7).

Unto the church of God which is at Corinth, to them that are sanctified in Christ Jesus, called to be saints [where he calls the members saints] (I Corinthians 1:2).

And all the brethren which are with me, unto the churches at Galatia (Galatians 1:2).

To the saints which are at Ephesus, and to the faithful in Christ (Ephesians 1:1).

To all the saints in Christ Jesus which are at Philippi (Philippians 1:1).

To the saints and faithful brethren in Christ which are at Colosse (Colossians 1:2).

Unto the church of the Thessalonians which is in God the Father and in the Lord Jesus Christ (1Thessalonians 1:1).

Each of these letters stress that Paul is writing to members of the church at each locale. He refers to the general members of the church as saints . . . not as people who had reached sainthood because of their greatness or accomplishments, but it is apparently the term used to describe each general member of the church. These saints were his converts, the ones he had brought into the church on his visits there. In some cases they had apparently written him seeking his counsel on some doctrinal points of the gospel he had preached to them. And on others, word had come to him of the practices they had fallen into that were contrary to the things he had taught them. His letters to them addressed these situations.

There is critical danger that can occur when we assume to understand the answers, when in fact we don't even know the questions. Paul and these members spoke a common doctrinal language. When he said certain things to them, they could relate, because it was either in answer to their questions, or it was in regard to practices they were following. Therefore, if we, a couple of millennia later, try to pick up a book, and without an extensive background knowledge of those people, or of the practices in which they were involved, expect to fully understand a bunch of answers, when we don't have any idea as to the nature of the questions that were asked, we stand in serious jeopardy of assuming incorrect information. However, if the practices were the same ones that we were practicing today, and we had an understanding of the same doctrines, there would not be a communication gap. That is precisely what the Apostle Peter was trying to warn those of us who would read the Bible in the last days of, concerning Paul's writings. These writings for all practical intents and purposes might as well be in a foreign language as far as the common man is concerned. In short; the Bible was written "for" everybody, but it wasn't written "to" everybody. Those who assume the intent of many of Paul's statements, according to Peter, run the risk of misunderstanding, and a possible loss of their salvation as a result.

11. *Behold, the days come, saith the Lord God, that I will send a famine in the land, not a famine of bread, nor a thirst for water, but of hearing the words of the Lord:*

12. *And they shall wander from sea to sea, and from the north even to the east, they shall run to and fro to seek the word of the Lord, and shall not find it.*

—Amos 8:11-12

CHAPTER 14
APOSTASY AND DARKNESS

The Savior spent three years trying to instruct the twelve Apostles concerning how to run the kingdom (Church), after His departure. He instructed them and gave them the keys of the Melchizedek Priesthood so they would be authorized to officiate in his stead (see Luke 24:48-50). After the crucifixion of the Savior, Peter and the rest of the Twelve, which was now eleven because Judas hung himself after betraying Christ, met to decide what they should do next. They seem to have been somewhat at a loss for the whole of that which the Savior had been preparing them for, as witnessed by the account of John:

> *There were together, Simon Peter, and Thomas called Didymus, and Nathanael of Cana in Galilee, and the sons of Zebedee, and two other of his disciples. Simon Peter saith unto them, I go a fishing. They say unto him, We also go with thee. They went forth, and entered into a ship immediately (John 21:2-3).*

Before being called as an apostle by the Savior, Peter had been a fisherman by trade, and it would appear that he was going back to that original trade. Kind of like he was saying, it's been a great ride for the past three years, but I guess it's over and I'd better get back to earning a living. But the Master returned from the grave in His resurrected state, and got them back on track, instructing them to move the work forward through missionary work.

However, the first item of business was to keep the Quorum of the Twelve Apostles intact, by replacing Judas. We have documentation of that fact in the account recorded in the Book of Acts:

> And they appointed two, Joseph called Barsabas, who was surnamed Justus, and Matthias.
>
> And they prayed, and said, thou, Lord, which knowest the hearts of all men, shew whether of these two thou hast chosen, that he may take part of this ministry and apostleship, from which Judas by transgression fell, that he might go to his own place.
>
> And they gave forth their lots; and the lot fell upon Matthias; and he was numbered with the eleven apostles (Acts 1:23-26).

Why did they need to replace Judas? Because that is the way that the Savior established His Church while He was upon the earth. He called a quorum of twelve (symbolic of the twelve tribes of Israel), and later as the need arose, he called more men and ordained them to the quorum of the Seventy (see Luke 10:1), to assist the Apostles in the work.

The topic of church organization is all important, in that the Savior set it up the way he wanted it to be run, as it says:

> Now therefore ye are no more strangers and foreigners, but fellow citizens with the saints, and of the household of God;
>
> And are built upon the foundation of apostles and prophets, Jesus Christ himself being the chief cornerstone;
>
> In whom all the building fitly framed together groweth unto an holy temple unto the Lord:
>
> In whom ye also are builded together for an habitation of God through the Spirit (Ephesians 2:19-22).

The Savior here likens the structure of His Church organization to a building. Anyone who has ever been associated with the building industry knows that the building is only as strong as its foundation. If the foundation is weak, the building will eventually crumble and fall. Notice who Christ said would be the foundation of His church? That's right, prophets and apostles, with Jesus Christ being the cornerstone, the point at which the entire building is held together.

In light of this information, I would submit to you that if His truly authorized church is on the earth today, it will need to be run by a prophet, and twelve apostles, with other men called to assist the work as needed, namely the Seventy as Jesus did in the original church (see Luke 10:1). The apostle Paul reprimanded the church at Corinth, for their deviation from the set doctrinal path laid down by the Savior for His Church:

> Now I beseech you brethren, by the name of our Lord Jesus Christ, that ye all speak the same thing, and that there be no divisions among you; but that ye be perfectly joined together in the same mind and in the same judgment.
>
> For it hath been declared unto me of you, my brethren, by them, which are of the house of Chloe, that there are contentions among you.
>
> Now this I say, that every one of you saith, I am of Paul; and I of Apollos; and I of Cephas (Peter); and I of Christ.
>
> Is Christ divided? Was Paul crucified for you? or were ye baptized in the name of Paul?
>
> I thank God that I baptized none of you, but Crispus and Gaius; Lest any should say that I had baptized in mine own name (1 Corinthians 1:10-15).

That is a fairly stinging rebuke to receive from one of the Lord's anointed servants. And why was he so upset? Because Paul saw that they were changing the pattern and doctrines that the Savior had established as necessary for salvation. Meanwhile, in Ephesians, Paul further illuminates the reason for the organizational structure of his church. "And he gave some, apostles; and some, prophets; and some evangelists; and some, pastors and teachers." And why did he set it up that way? "For the perfecting of the saints, for the work of the ministry, and for the edifying of the body of Christ (members of the church)." (Ephesians 4:11-12) I don't know about you, but I have yet to meet anyone who has achieved perfection here in this life. "Till we all come in the unity of faith," with literally thousands of different Christian sects dotting the land, it's obvious that we're not quite there yet.

And the knowledge of the Son of God, unto a perfect man, unto the measure of the stature of the fullness of Christ: that we henceforth be no more children, tossed to and fro, and carried about with every wind of doctrine, by the sleight of men, and cunning craftiness, whereby they lie in wait to deceive (Ephesians 4:13-14).

It sounds to me as if that organization needs to still exist for a while longer at least, because we still have need for guidance in those specified areas of concern. Paul further warns us of seducing doctrines that will exist among us in the last days:

This know also, that in the last days perilous times shall come. For men shall be lovers of their own selves, covetous, boasters, proud, blasphemers, disobedient to parents, unthankful, unholy,

Without natural affection, trucebreakers, false accusers, incontinent, fierce, despisers of those that are good,

Traitors, heady, highminded, lovers of pleasures more than lovers of God;

Having a form of godliness; but denying the power thereof: from such turn away (2 Timothy 3:1-5).

For the time will come when they will not endure sound doctrine; but after their own lusts shall they heap to themselves teachers, having itching ears;

And they shall turn away their ears from the truth, and shall be turned unto fables (2 Timothy 4:3-4).

Paul understood the problems that would exist with the corrupting of the pure doctrines that he taught, and the minimizing of the proper priesthood authority, and tried to warn us of them. So what are we to do? For every person, there can be a different interpretation. But Peter warned us as stated earlier at the end of chapter 13, of the danger of misinterpretations of Paul's teachings. Enter... the book of Joseph (Mormon). The teachings of the Bible have been twisted and distorted by different people, for centuries now. But there is a second witness, one that hasn't been subjected to the re-translation and loss of integrity in which the Bible has. It is the second witness for the truths that the Bible contains. When used side-by-side as a companion to the Bible, it unmistakably establishes the doctrines, so they cannot be twisted, or misinterpreted. Let me cite an example of this.

The Old Testament records the story of Adam and Eve in the Garden of Eden, where the couple partakes of the forbidden fruit, and are banished from the garden. All we are told is that God told them to multiply and replenish the earth, and that in the day they ate of the tree of the knowledge of good and evil they would become subject to physical death. The serpent beguiles them and they eat the fruit, and are cast out of the garden, thus bringing mortality upon themselves and their posterity after them. The only other thing we have is about them bearing children.

The Book of Mormon record however, reveals the following:

And after Adam and Eve had partaken of the forbidden fruit they were driven out of the garden of Eden, to till the earth.

And they have brought forth children; yea, even the family of all the earth.

And now, behold, if Adam had not transgressed he would not have fallen, but he would have remained in the garden of Eden. And all things, which were created must have remained in the same state in which they were after they were created; and they must have remained forever, and had no end.

And they would have had no children; wherefore they would have remained in a state of innocence, having no joy, for they knew no misery; doing no good, for they knew no sin.

But behold, all things have been done in the wisdom of him who knoweth all things.

Adam fell that men might be; and men are that they might have joy.

And the Messiah cometh in the fullness of time, that he may redeem the children of men from the fall. And because that they are redeemed from the fall they have become free forever, knowing good from evil; to act for themselves and not to be acted on, save it be by the punishment of the law at the great and last day, according to the commandments which God hath given. Wherefore men are free according to the flesh; and all things are given unto them, which are expedient unto man (2 Nephi 2:19-20, 22-27).

We also learn from the book of Moses, which was also revealed to Joseph Smith, how Adam and Eve felt about their decision to partake of the fruit and give up their life of innocent bliss.

And in that day the Holy Ghost fell upon Adam, which beareth record of the Father and the Son, saying: I am the only begotten of the Father from the beginning, henceforth and forever, that as thou hast fallen thou mayest be redeemed, and all mankind, even as many as will.

And in that day Adam blessed God and was filled, and began to prophesy concerning all the families of the earth, saying: Blessed be the name of God, for because of my transgression my eyes are opened, and in this life I shall have joy, and again in the flesh I shall see God.

And Eve, his wife, heard all these things and was glad, saying: Were it not for our transgression we never should have had seed, and never should have had known good and evil, and the joy of our redemption, and the eternal life which God giveth to all the obedient.

And Adam and Eve blessed the name of God, and they made all things known unto their sons and daughters (Moses 5:9-12).

As we can see, with these additional insights, a whole new light is cast on one of the most pivotal of all Christian doctrines. It turns what from the Bible seems to be a negative act, into a fall forward, not backward. This position leads to other Latter-day Saint doctrine, which will be examined in chapter 16, concerning salvation.

After the death and resurrection of the Savior, wicked men, who opposed Christianity, sought, and eventually took the lives of every member of the Twelve except for the Apostle John, who was exiled to the isle of Patmos, before realizing the promise made to him by the Savior, of being able to remain on the earth until the second coming. The result of this wickedness was that they could not get back together to select replacements as they had after the death of Judas. What was the end result? The loss of the Savior's priesthood authority from the earth. This period of time is what many call the dark ages, or the Great Apostasy.

Old Testament prophets had prophesied of this day:

> *Behold, the days come, saith the Lord God, that I will send a famine in the land, not a famine of bread, nor a thirst for water, but of hearing of the words of the Lord: And they shall wander from sea to sea, and from the north even to the east, they shall run to and fro to seek the word of the Lord, and shall not find it (Amos 8:11-12).*

Why would they not be able to find it? Because the servants who held the keys of the Melchizedek Priesthood were no longer on the earth. Many of the saints in Thessalonica were concerned that the second coming of the Messiah would be somewhere in the near future, and Paul addressed those concerns:

> *Now we beseech you, brethren, by the coming of our Lord Jesus Christ, and our gathering together unto him,*
>
> *That ye be not soon shaken in mind, or be troubled, neither by spirit, nor by word, nor by letter as from us, as that the day of Christ is at hand.*
>
> *Let no man deceive you by any means: for that day shall not come, except there come a falling away (Apostacia-Greek form) first, and that man of sin be revealed, the son of perdition (2 Thessalonians 2:1-3).*

There we have it, there was going to be a falling away from the truth, and a famine of God's word (and His authority), before the second coming happens. That would seem to mean that this apostasy has already either happened, as believed by the Church of Jesus Christ of Latter-day Saints, or that it is yet to happen still somewhere in the future. Either way if, it is to be taken from the earth, then it has got to be restored to the earth before the second advent of the promised Messiah. We turn to the book of Acts for the answer. After the day of Pentecost, when the promise of the comforter was finally fulfilled, Peter and John were preaching the gospel, during a missionary journey and after healing a man, lame from birth, they counseled:

Repent ye therefore, and be converted, that your sins may be blotted out, when the times of refreshing shall come from the presence of the Lord;

And he shall send Jesus Christ, which before was preached unto you:

Whom the heaven must receive until the restitution (restoration) of all things, which God hath spoken by the mouth of all his holy prophets, since the world began (Acts 3:19-21).

The restitution of what things? All things! Every major practice and covenant that was part of the gospel from the very beginning.

If the gospel in its fullness was truly taken from the earth, only God himself, or His beloved son, the Messiah and Savior of the world could restore it. As mentioned in chapter twelve, no man could take the priesthood to himself. Someone who holds the authority to do so must bestow it upon his head. It is the testimony of the Latter-day Saints that that is precisely what has happened. Along with that priesthood authority, the saving ordinances of the Melchizedek Priesthood have been restored. Within the sacred walls of holy temples baptisms for the dead are performed. This is done by those still living, by proxy. This might sound like a strange practice, but it was a part of the Lord's gospel, anciently: "Else what shall they do which are baptized for the dead, if the dead rise not at all, why are they then baptized for the dead?" (1 Corinthians 15:29). As we can see, this was a practice in the original church. Latter-day Saints believe that just as Peter said, when a person dies, and leaves this life without having had a chance to hear the gospel taught in its fullness, he/she will be afforded that opportunity in the spirit world (see 1 Peter 3:18-20; 4:5-6).

Many point to the story of Christ and the two malefactors on the cross (see Luke 23:39-43), as a support for deathbed repentance. They claim that the profession that he made to the one that he would be with him that day in Paradise, is evidence that he was promised an inheritance in heaven. However, the Latter-day Saints would cite the references from Peter, as evidence that Christ didn't go to heaven that day. They believe that Christ went to the spirit world to prepare the way for the teaching of those deceased souls who were awaiting the gospel message (see 1 Peter 3:18-20; 4:5-6). When the Savior appeared to Mary in the garden, she rushed to embrace him, but he told her: "Touch me not; for I am not yet ascended to my father" (see John 20: 1-17). The Savior obviously didn't go with the malefactor to heaven that day, because three days later he still had not been where his father was. Peter is speaking of where Christ was during the time between his death and resurrection, the spirit world. Once those spirits have accepted the gospel message, people here can go to one of the holy temples and, by proxy, perform those ordinances for them, thus entitling them to receive the blessings of membership in Christ's Church beyond the grave.

The crowning ordinance performed in the temples, is that of celestial marriage. Latter-day Saints believe that marriage between a man and a woman is the highest calling and respon-sibility we as mortals have in this life. Once we have been given our physical body, and have gone through our youth and adoles-cence, learning and receiving the saving ordinances of salvation, our responsibility is to give other of our Heavenly Father's spirit children the opportunity to obtain their physical bodies. We are then required to raise them to the best of our ability, to learn and obey the commandments so they can also return back into their Father's kingdom after their mortal life has ended.

Men, who have been given those priesthood keys seal couples and families, together, for time and for all eternity. What an absolutely exulting doctrine! That a marriage, and family relationship doesn't have to end with: "Till death do we part," but instead be continued beyond this life . . . into the eternities with the Father and the Son.

And what of those who have departed this life and have not had this sealing ordinance performed for them? Couples can go to the temple, and again, act as proxy for them that are deceased. These ordinances are physical ordinances, so as spirits in the postmortal world, they are incapable of performing them for themselves. That is the doctrine with which the Prophet Malachi concluded the Old Testament:

Behold, I will send you Elijah the prophet before the coming of the great and dreadful day of the Lord:

And he shall turn the heart of the fathers to the children, and the heart of the children to their fathers, lest I come and smite the earth with a curse (Malachi 4:5-6).

On April 3, 1836, this prophecy was fulfilled. As Joseph Smith was attending to the affairs of the Lord in the temple at Kirtland, Ohio, Elijah appeared to Joseph and restored upon him the keys of God's sealing authority.

Through genealogy work, seeking out our kindred dead, we can ascertain who have received these ordinances, and who have not. Once they have been performed for them, if they accept the gospel in the spirit world when it is taught to them, it will be in full force in their behalf. Why wouldn't a loving Heavenly Father, want to give all of his children an equal opportunity to make it back into his presence? These and other vital ordinances are all part of the restoration of all things, and exist today through the ministrations of servants who hold the Holy Priesthood.

20. *And he shall send Jesus Christ, which before was preached unto you:*

21. *Whom the heaven must receive until the times of restitution of all things, which God hath spoken by the mouth of all his holy prophets since the world began.*

—Acts 3:20-21

CHAPTER 15
A DAY OF RESTORATION

After centuries of turmoil and strife over religion, the time had finally arrived to begin the final phase of this whole grand story of the gathering of Israel. Darkness and Apostasy had covered the land long enough! People had been put to death in the name of religion, from during the dark ages, to the Crusades, and finally, to what would come to become known as the American Revolution. The Lord was now ready to set his hand a second time to recover His covenant people, and reestablish the covenants that He had made with their forefathers thousands of years earlier. It began with what is referred to as "the Reformation ." However there is a major difference in the terms: reformation and restoration. To reform is to make changes in something that already exists, but something must have already existed and then have been lost or removed in order to be able to restore it.

If the church and its priesthood authority really had been taken from the earth as the Bible says it would be, there would need to be a restoration of those things, not just a reformation. It would also of necessity require God himself to authorize such an event. Inspired men such as Martin Luther, John Huss, Zwingli, Calvin, and others, felt a stirring in their souls, to break the death grip that had been imposed upon them. Luther said that religion had gone astray, but that he recognized that he lacked the authority to do anything about it. He did, however, feel duty bound to expose the things that he had discovered from holy writ that were not as the Savior had outlined. He made his famous list, which he tacked to a door, in protest, and thus began that reformation. We all know the rest of the story. It culminated in the revolt of thousands of inspired patriots, who, following those stirrings of the Holy Ghost, migrated to this, the American continent, in their quest for religious freedom. The desire to worship, "how, where, or what they may" burned within their breasts, and they had the courage to follow those promptings, to this new land. It was to be a land of promise choice above all others.

Does that phrase ring a bit familiar? Well it should. Earlier, in the first few chapters of this work, I discussed the fact that God had made a covenant first with Abraham, and finally with Joseph. They were promised that their posterity would be as numerous as the sands of the sea, or the stars in the heaven. That posterity would be given a new land, one that was choice above all others, in which they could worship the Lord, their God, in peace. They were told that even though because of wickedness they would be scattered and smitten, He would not forsake nor forget them, but remember the covenants that He had made with their forefathers. That in the last days, through the chosen birthright tribe of Joseph (through Ephraim), He would restore truth and light to the earth, and set His hand a second time to recover His lost and fallen people. And that Christ would reign supreme upon the earth, for a thousand years, with them in His presence, as their King, and their God. But with the conditions that existed in the world at the time of the reformation that could not happen. So it was that these great, inspired men led a revolt against religious tyranny, and a new day dawned. In 1776, the inspired writers of the Declaration of Independence penned the document that would declare to all the world that the promised time had come.

At the turn of the century, America was just beginning to spread her wings with this newfound freedom. There was a religious awakening in this great land that saw the creation of many new religious sects come to be. People were caught up in the spirit of the whole movement, and sought to align themselves with the many various denominations, and religious zeal was rampant! Many and varied were their doctrines, and great was their enthusiasm for this newfound religious freedom. However, there was one major problem that somehow the leaders of these sects failed to recognize, "no man taketh this honor unto himself, but he that is called of God as was Aaron" (Hebrews 5:4).

The will was there, but what about the authority to act in God's name, and have it recognized by Him as binding? The right to this sacred task belonged to Ephraim, and to his seed, to preside at the head of the Church. What of them? And what of the Melchizedek Priesthood, which was to be the power of God in this whole winding up scene in the world's history? Well in the midst of all of this zeal and confusion, one young man asked himself those very questions. He was only fourteen years old at the time, but was involved very deeply in the search for the true religion... you know... the one that the Savior set up. The one true way described in the New Testament that was truly authorized by him to offer the ordinances of salvation, and have them recognized by him. With the differences of opinion offered on the part of these different parties of religionists, he was totally confused. He was leaning toward affiliating himself with the Methodist sect, although others of his family had aligned themselves with the Presbyterians. He would seek out the clergy of these different sects and ask them questions regarding the things he would read in the Bible. He was confused because their answers seemed to disagree and contradict each other, and none of them rang true to his soul. He pondered seriously on the matter, not knowing quite what to do. Then one day as he was reading the New Testament, he came upon some verses that seemed to jump out at him. One particular passage impressed him very deeply: "If any of you lack wisdom, let him ask of God, that giveth to all men liberally, and upbraideth not; and it shall be given him. But let him ask in faith, nothing wavering" (James 1:5-6).

It entered into every feeling of his heart, and he pondered on it continually. At length he decided to act upon it, and take the scriptures at their word. He gave the following account:

> *It was on the morning of a beautiful, clear day, early in the spring of 1820. It was the first time in my life that I had made such an attempt, for amidst all my anxieties I had never as yet made the attempt to pray vocally*

He then tells of an experience that would change the course of mankind.

> *After I had retired to the place I had previously designed to go, having looked around me, and finding myself alone, I kneeled down and began to offer up the desires of my heart to God. I had scarcely done so, when immediately I was seized upon by some power which entirely overcame me, and had such an astonishing influence over me as to bind my tongue so that I could not speak.*

Satan, knowing of what was about to transpire, was apparently trying to stop it by destroying this young man. He continues:

> *At the very moment when I was ready to sink into despair and abandon myself to destruction. . . just at this moment of great alarm, I saw a pillar of light exactly over my head, above the brightness of the sun, which descended gradually until it fell upon me. It no sooner appeared than I found myself delivered from the enemy, which held me bound. When the light rested upon me I saw two personages, whose brightness and glory defy all description, standing in the air. One of them spake unto me, calling me by name and said, pointing to the other . . . This is my beloved son. Hear him!*

He concludes the experience by saying that he was told that he was not to join any of the churches of the day, but instead he was going to be the instrument by which the true and living Church of Jesus Christ would be restored to the earth, in its fullness, containing all of its authority. He was told that while all of the churches had truth, none of them had His authorization, which is so critical when acting in His name. After a four-year period, in which he was tried and tested, the gospel was finally returned to the earth, in its fullness.

On April 6, 1830, the formal establishing of the Church of Jesus Christ of Latter-day Saints was finalized, and officially recognized by the state of New York. The priesthood of God was restored to the earth. First the Aaronic Priesthood, by the hands of the resurrected John the Baptist. And later, the Melchizedek Priesthood, by Peter, James, and John, Christ's ancient Apostles. These ancient servants appeared to the Prophet Joseph Smith and conferred these two priesthoods upon his head, and authorized him to begin the process of restoring the Savior's church to the earth. That Church has grown steadily since that time, and has been taken by its missionaries to practically every nation and continent on the earth. With the restoration of the Holy Priesthood of God to the earth, the Savior has also called a Prophet and Twelve Apostles . . . who stand as His special witnesses to all the world of the Savior and His divinity. They continue to lead the Lord's saints in these latter-days, just as His ancient apostles guided His saints in ancient times. The ordinances of salvation are in full-force, and available through His authorized servants, to all who wish to humble themselves, and follow Him.

That is the testimony of the Church of Jesus Christ of Latter-day Saints. Pure and simple: either Joseph Smith was a Prophet of the Living God, or he was not. The Book of Mormon is either the missing Stick of Joseph, or it is not. Both of these claims hinge upon each other. True prophets don't bring forth false books, and likewise, false prophets don't bring forth true books. If one is true, the other is also, for they are inseparable. Challenges of individual doctrines are of no consequence, because if it is the Church of Christ as we claim, then all of the doctrines and interpretations are true as well, no matter what they might be. It would appear that the Book of Mormon is not the one on trial here. It is the word of God, and will stand on its own merit. Therefore it is each of us who are really on trial, before God, to see if we will be true enough to put this sacred record to the test.

Moroni, the last prophet to write in the book, gives this challenge to the world:

> And when ye shall receive these things, I would exhort you
> that ye would ask God, the Eternal Father, in the name of

Christ, if these things are not true; and if ye will ask with a sincere heart, with real intent, having faith in Christ, he will manifest the truth of it unto you by the power of the Holy Ghost. And by the power of the Holy Ghost ye may know the truth of all things (Moroni 10:4).

Isn't it comforting to know that we don't have to just rely on other people's testimonials in order for us to know the truth? But we can actually know the truth for ourselves.

The crowning point of the Book of Mormon is its account of the visit of the Savior to the people on the American continent shortly after His death and resurrection. It tells of Him ministering to them, and promising to return to earth in a coming day to reign on the earth. In the book of Third Nephi He tells the Nephites that they are the other sheep that He had told the Jews of (see John 10:16). Chapters 20-24 and 29-30 of Third Nephi are rich in information on the history of the house of Israel, and reiterates the fact that they are the fulfillment of the promise made to Abraham and Jacob; that in the last days their records would come forth to reclaim scattered Israel.

I add my witness to that of Moroni, that the Book of Mormon is truly the word of God, and the missing book of the tribe of Joseph, prophesied of by Ezekiel, many millennia ago. I challenge all to read it and inquire of God as to its truthfulness. Millions have already done so, and millions more will do it before He comes again in His glory, to say the work is done. It seems to me that one has nothing to lose by trying this simple experiment. Unless you know the whereabouts of Joseph's record it could be a near fatal mistake to disregard the possibility of the truthfulness of our claims.

18. *Yea, a man may say, Thou hast faith, and I have works: shew me thy faith without thy works, and I will shew thee my faith by my works.*

19. *Thou believest that there is one God: thou doest well: the devils also believe, and tremble.*

20. *But what wilt thou know, O vain man, that faith without works is dead?*

24. *Ye see then how that by works a man is justified, and not by faith only.*

—James 2:18-20, 24

CHAPTER 16

THE DOCTRINE OF SALVATION

One of the major differences in Latter-day Saint doctrine from that of the conventional Christian world is our concept concerning the conditions that we will encounter once we leave mortality and return to the world of spirits. I have been asked on more than one occasion about the doctrine of the Church in regard to "being saved." One person put it to me this way: "So Mormons believe that we aren't saved by grace as the Bible states, but that we have to earn our way there through our good deeds?" I have to admit that is an interesting way of putting it, and one that is not entirely true. It is not so cut and dried as that. Let me first state before attempting to shed light on this pivotal doctrine, that none of us must ever forget the terrible price that was paid by our elder brother in ransoming us from certain damnation in the Garden of Gethsemane, on the cross at Calvary, and finished in His triumphant resurrection from the garden tomb on the third day following His crucifixion. That atonement for sin offered so freely by the Savior of the world, is nevertheless, not free. He bought us with his blood, and that price was a very high one indeed. The Atonement was the single most important event in the history of this universe. Because of that sacrifice we will be eternally indebted to Him. Latter-day

Saints believe that it was an infinite atonement, and is available to all mankind, from the greatest to the least. The fact that it is available to all doesn't necessarily mean that it will be used by all. There is a difference between believing and becoming. I may know that going on a regular exercise program will improve my health, but unless I actually do something about it and exercise, all of my belief will avail me nothing. The weight will not just magically melt off, and my body won't receive the physical benefits of exercise merely because I believed in it.

The Jews at the time of Christ were fanatical concerning the law of Moses. So much so in fact, that they didn't recognize the Messiah when He came. Everything that God gave to Israel in the law of Moses was symbolic of the coming of the promised Messiah, and was meant to prepare them for His mortal advent. When Jesus came, He told the people that the law of Moses had served its purpose, and that it was now to be fulfilled in him. They actually used the law to put Him to death. Many have used the teachings of Paul to support the idea that the gift of the Atonement is free to us merely upon our profession of faith in Jesus Christ.

The second chapter of the book of James is unmistakably clear in renouncing such a doctrine.

> *Even so faith, if it hath not works is dead, being alone.*
>
> *Yea, a man may say, Thou hast faith, and have works: shew me thy faith without thy works, and I will show thee my faith by my works.*
>
> *Thou believest that there is one God; thou doest well: the devils also believe and tremble.*
>
> *But wilt thou know O vain man, that faith without works is dead.*
>
> *Was not Abraham our father justified by works, when he had offered Isaac his son upon the altar? (James 2:17-21).*

The Jewish religious hierarchy at the time of Christ made their livelihood from the offerings contained in the law of Moses. When the Savior came, and announced that the law was no longer needed, but was fulfilled with a higher law, they risked losing their main source of income. They continued to preach to the people that they must continue in the law of Moses.

After Christ had raised Lazarus from the dead, they met to plot his death. This final miracle was irrefutable evidence that He held the power over life and death, so the Jewish leaders plotted his death:

> Then gathered the chief priests, and the Pharisees a council, and said What do we? for this man doeth many miracles.
>
> If we let him thus alone, all men will believe on him: and the Romans shall come and take away both our place and our nation (John 11:47-48).

After the crucifixion the leaders continued to push the law as the most important aspect of their worship. When we discussed the law of Moses earlier in Chapter 12, I pointed out that it was in conjunction with the Aaronic Priesthood, and contained the lesser ordinances of salvation. Later, in chapters 14 and 15, we discussed the Melchizedek Priesthood, which contained the higher ordinances of the gospel of Christ. It was of these that the Savior was referring to when He said that the law was fulfilled. It had served its purpose, bringing Israel to the time of His ministry.

Throughout the New Testament, Gospel writers, especially the Apostle Paul, were constantly addressing the Jewish obsession with the law of Moses. Examples of his frustration with their apparent lack of ability to leave the law behind, and move ahead with the higher ordinances are found in his epistles.

> Knowing that a man is not justified by the works of the law, but by the faith of Jesus Christ, even we have believed in Jesus Christ, that we might be justified by the faith of Christ, and not by the works of the law: for by the works of the law shall no man be justified . . .
>
> I do not frustrate the grace of God: for if righteousness come by the law, then Christ is dead in vain (Galatians 2:16, 21).
>
> For by grace are ye saved through; and that not of your-selves: it is the gift of God:
>
> Not of works lest any man should boast.

For we are his workmanship, created in Christ Jesus unto good works, which God hath before ordained that we should walk in them (Ephesians 2:8-10).

Many have interpreted these passages as saying that we are saved by our faith only, not according to our good works, when in reality he is referring to the works of the law of Moses, which they were so blindly tied to. Under the law there was very little personal growth for an individual, because they were told every move to make, and when to make it. When these Jewish Christians joined Christ's Church, they were trying to still keep the law of Moses with them, and Paul therefore explicitly tells them the error of that, by explaining to them that the works of the law don't have the power to save them unto salvation. That they needed to leave the old behind, and now put their faith in Jesus Christ, and do the works that he had now ordained unto all of us to do (see 3 Nephi 15:2-10).

To understand the true value and place of works in our salvation process, let me attempt to put it as simply as possible. Someday we will all have to stand before our Maker and account for our lives, be they good or evil. Contrary to all the "St. Peter at the Pearly Gates" jokes, it is Christ who is the keeper of the gate, and whom we will all have to answer to (see John 5:22). Nephi adds his witness to that of John:

O then, my beloved brethren, come unto the Lord, the Holy One. Remember that his paths are righteous. Behold the way for man is narrow, but it lieth in a straight course before him, and the keeper of the gate is the Holy One of Israel; and he employeth no servant there; and there is none other way save it be by the gate; for he cannot be deceived, for the Lord God is his name (2 Nephi 9:41).

It doesn't appear to be what we did or didn't do while on earth that will be the deciding factor in what eternal rewards we receive, but rather who we are, when we stand before him. And who we are is largely determined by what we have done with our lives. We are all products of our environment, and those of us who have lost our lives in the service of others, will find our lives. It is in the doing that the true growth comes, and we experience the things that will mold us into the finished product that we came to earth to learn to become. If we have done the works that Paul said God has created us to do during the course of our lives, we will be able to stand in His presence without shame, guilt, or regret when that Day of Judgment comes. Faith is definitely the beginning of our salvation. But it is our works that is the finisher of it.

Steven Robinson, who has written such books as *Believing Christ* and *Following Christ*, elaborates on the concept of being saved by grace. He said that the concept of Hellenism was introduced by Alexander, and was individual based. It's what everybody else is doing individually. Judaism was based on people collectively. Paul was speaking from a Judaic viewpoint. When he says "us" and "we," he is speaking of the Church. The prophet Joseph Smith said that in Paul's writings to the Romans concerning justification, the word "freely" should be translated "only" (see Romans 3:23-24, 28). We have all sinned, and are justified upon conditions of repentance, only through the grace of Christ. It was the Roman saint's faith in the Messiah, not their diligence in keeping the works of the law that would allow them to be cleansed from their sinful and fallen state. The prophet Alma says in the Book of Mormon, that man cannot merit anything on his own works (see Alma 22:14), it must be on the merits of Christ (see Moroni 6:4). When we come to earth to begin our mortal experience we fall from the presence of God. We can't earn our way to Heaven, so how are we to get back? The Pharisees and the Sadducees were trying to return to the Lord's presence through the works of the law of Moses. Thus when the Savior told them that it was impossible (remember, salvation didn't come from the ordinances of the Aaronic Priesthood, but those of the Melchizedek), they were infuriated. The prophet Nephi tells us that it was what Christ did, not what we do that will allow us to return to God, and dwell in His presence (see 2 Nephi 2:8).

In the same chapter, verses five and six he testifies that it is impossible to be saved by the works of the law of Moses. Other prophets agree with him, and Paul stressed that it is only through Christ that we may obtain salvation. However it is Nephi who puts the concept of being saved by grace into its true perspective:

> *Wherefore, for this cause hath the Lord God promised unto me that these things that I write shall be kept and preserved, and handed down unto my seed, from generation to generation, that the promise may be fulfilled unto Joseph, that his seed should never perish as long as the earth shall stand.*
>
> *Wherefore these things shall go forth from generation to generation as long as the earth shall stand; and they shall go according to the will and pleasure of God; and the Nations who shall possess them shall be judged of them according to the words, which are written.*
>
> *For we labor diligently to write, to persuade our children, and also our brethren, to believe in Christ, and to be reconciled to God; for we know that it is by grace that we are saved, after all we can do.*
>
> *And not withstanding we believe in Christ, we keep the law of Moses, and look forward with steadfastness unto Christ, until the law shall be fulfilled.*
>
> *For, for this end was the law given; wherefore the law hath become dead unto us, and we are made alive in Christ because of our faith; yet we keep the law because of the commandments.*
>
> *And we talk of Christ, we rejoice in Christ, we preach of Christ, we prophesy of Christ, and we write according to our prophecies, that our children may know to what source they may look for a remission of their sins (2 Nephi 25:21-26).*

I believe that he said it in the simplest terms when he said: "We are saved by grace . . . after all we can do." To further clarify our beliefs concerning this doctrine, and bring to light what the Apostle Paul is trying to get across to us, I am going to again return to some of the thoughts of Steven Robinson. We can be cleansed from our sins and saved by the power of the Savior . . . after all we can do. We have to do all that we can to become one with Christ, so that He will take away our guilt, and allow us to regain God's presence. The Book of Mormon teaches that the Savior does not redeem men "in their sins" (see Alma 11:34; Helaman 5:10). "The wicked remain as though there had been no redemption made, except it be the losing of the bands of death" (Alma 11:41). The Savior came to redeem men "from their sins because of repentance, and upon the conditions of repentance" (Helaman 5:11).

Elder Dallin H. Oaks of the Quorum of the Twelve Apostles has said:

> "What do these basic principles mean in the case of a lax Latter-day Saint who deliberately commits a serious transgression in the expectation that he or she will enjoy the effects or benefits of the sin now and then make a speedy and relatively painless repentance and soon be as good as new?"

He then elaborates on the price we must pay to obtain the blessings of the atonement, quoting also the Savior's words to us that I have alluded to in this chapter (see Doctrine and Covenants 19:15-20). Then he continues,

> "As we consider these sobering words of the Savior, we realize that there is something very peculiar about the state of mind or heart of the person who deliberately commits sin in the expectation that he or she will speedily and comfortably repent and continue as a servant of God, preaching repentance and asking others to come unto Christ. Am I suggesting that the benefits of the atonement are not available for the person who heedlessly sins? Of course not. But I am suggesting that there is a relationship between sin and suffering that is not understood by people who knowingly sin in the expectation that all the burden of suffering will be borne by another, that the sin is all theirs, but the suffering is all His. That is not the way. Repentance, which is an assured passage to an eternal destination, is nevertheless not a free ride" (BYU fireside, August 5, 1990).

President Spencer W. Kimball, a former prophet, had this to say about the relationship between our suffering for our misdeeds, and the Savior's forgiveness of them:

> "Suffering is a very important part of repentance. One has not begun to repent until he has suffered intensely for his sins . . . If a person hasn't suffered, he hasn't repented . . . He has got to go through a change in his system whereby he suffers, and then forgiveness is a possibility. Very frequently people think they have repented and are worthy of forgiveness when all they have done is express sorrow or regret at the unfortunate happening" (The Teachings of Spencer W. Kimball pp. 87, 88, 89).

96

Christ is going to be our advocate with the Father. Faithful doesn't mean perfect, as in marriage—in making and maintaining the covenants. We must place the Savior first, not second in our lives, and accept the things that He asks us to do whatever that may be. Our relationship with Him can't be vertical it must be horizontal. We must be on a level plane with Him in our conduct and deportment, striving to honor Him, and then He will profess us to the Father (see James 2:14; Romans 3:28). Paul and James use the words differently. In James 2:17-26, Paul defines faith as belief and behavior, but James defines it simply as belief, and behavior as works that must attend faith. If we accept faith as belief and behavior, can faith save us? Yes, because it will make us worthy to accept the saving grace of Christ, which will justify us. A great example of this is the story of Abraham and Isaac. If Abraham had said, I believe that it is God that wants me to sacrifice my son, but I'm not going to do it, would that have met God's criteria? Grace is like a newborn baby, God loves us first, then, we respond. Then he blesses us, and we respond again. He is always one up on us. One way to look at grace is to think of the feelings that we have for a newborn baby. What has that baby done for us to earn our love? Absolutely nothing! But the feelings we have for that infant are there just the same, and we would do anything in our power for it. That is how the Savior feels about us. We really can't do anything to warrant God's love, but He gives it to us just the same, because we are His children.

Brother Robinson also uses the example of a child who wants to buy a bicycle. The child works and saves, and works and saves in order to earn enough money to buy the treasured bike. After what seems like an eternity that child comes to his father and wants to go buy it. They go to the store and the father counts out the money that his child has worked so faithfully to earn, and sees that he is far short of the required amount. Because he has worked so diligently, and his heart was right in the matter, the Savior says, "Give me all you have, and I will make up the difference." I love this analogy! It rings true to me! The Savior doesn't require us to be truer than true, he just asks us to give Him all we have, and after we have done all that we can do, He will make up the difference. None of us is capable of paying the full price, so He takes our meager offering and multiplies it until it is sufficient to allow us entrance back into the presence of our Heavenly Father. This truly is the ultimate expression of grace, but to kid ourselves by thinking that we don't need to do anything to warrant that gift but simply believe in Him would appear to me to be nothing short of trampling on His sacred Atonement.

Before we close the topic of salvation, there are a few other aspects of it that we must, of necessity, explore. A common doctrinal belief of much of the Christian world is that we are all born into this world with the sin of Adam on our heads, and therefore are unclean until we are baptized. Baptism is indeed a necessary requirement for salvation as is illustrated in the third chapter of the gospel of John. When Nicodemus asked the Savior how a man could be born again, He answered him by saying that we all must be born of water and of the Spirit to receive eternal life (see John 3:5). Though that appears to be quite simple, in reality this simple doctrine has been diluted by the interpretations of men, as have many other doctrines. Surely something as essential to our salvation as this ordinance must be done precisely as the Savior instructed, not in some other way. Views today vary on this vital ordinance with some ascribing to immersion, some to sprinkling, and others even claiming that all that is required is to have a "baptism of the heart." Who is man to assume the right to change the doctrines and teachings of the Messiah? The teachings of the New Testament make it unmistakably clear that baptism is to be done by immersion, and by someone who holds the Holy Priesthood of God. Speaking of John the Baptist, the Apostle John said: "And John also was baptizing in Aenon near Salim, because there was much water there" (John 3:23). If baptisms were being performed by sprinkling, there would have been no need to seek a site with "much water there." The Apostle Paul further illustrates this principle in his epistles:

> *Know ye not, that so many of us as were baptized into Jesus Christ were baptized into his death? Therefore we are buried with him by baptism into death: but like as Christ was raised up from the dead by the glory of the Father, even so we also should walk in newness of life. For if we have been planted together in the likeness of his death, we shall be also in the likeness of his resurrection (Romans 6:3-5).*

> *Buried with him in baptism, wherein also ye are risen with him through the faith of the operation of God, who hath raised him from the dead (Colossians 2:12).*

According to Paul the ordinance of baptism is a symbolic gesture, on each of our parts, to the Savior that we are burying the former sinful person, and are coming forth as a new person, born again.

There are two elements that are present at our birth, we have been safe in an environment of water for nine months. When it is time for our birth, we come forth out of the water, a new, living, breathing human being. The other element is blood. In order to bring us into the world and give us life, our mothers must pass through the valley of the shadow of death. It is through their selfless sacrifice, which requires them to sacrifice their blood, that we have life. What a marvelous parallel between our first birth, and our rebirth! When we understand what the principle of baptism symbolizes, it becomes very apparent that it must be done by immersion. We must be immersed completely in a watery grave, putting to death the sinful person, in order to come forth anew. The practice of sprinkling, as we can see, would symbolize nothing. If we are truly born again, we will be a different person, and we will feel differently about the kind of life we wish to live. A Book of Mormon prophet describes this rebirth:

> *Yea, we believe all the words which thou hast spoken unto us; and also, we know of their surety and truth, because of the Spirit of the Lord Omnipotent, which has wrought a mighty change in us, or in our hearts, that we have no more disposition to do evil, but to do good continually (Mosiah 5:2).*

Many people say that Latter-day Saints believe in a different

God than the rest of the Christian world. Well, when it comes to this doctrine, that statement would apply. The God that we believe in, the one I have just described, is one of compassion, one, who wants each of His children to have all that He can possibly give to them.

He does not hold one person responsible for another person's acts. We believe that little children are alive in Christ, as are those who are mentally handicapped, and are not fully unaccountable for their actions. We believe that having just come from the presence of God, they are as perfect as one can possibly be in this life, and therefore, to teach that they are sinners, or treat them as such would be an error of major proportions. Many a parent has lost a child in infancy or young childhood without them having been baptized, and have been devastated when told that their child has been assigned to Hell because of their lack of baptism. Shortly after the ancient prophet Mormon ordained his son Moroni to the Ministry, he gave him the following concerning this practice:

> *And now, my son, I speak unto you concerning that which grieveth me exceedingly; for it grieveth me that there should disputations rise among you.*
>
> *For, if I have learned the truth, there have been disputations among you concerning the baptism of your little children.*
>
> *And now my son, I desire that ye should labor diligently, that this gross error should be removed from among you; for, for this intent I have written this epistle.*
>
> *For immediately after I had learned these things of you I inquired of the Lord concerning the matter. And the word of the Lord came to me by the power of the Holy Ghost, saying:*
>
> *Listen to the words of Christ, your redeemer, your Lord, and your God. Behold, I came into the world not to call the righteous but the sinners to repentance; the whole need no physician, but they that are sick; wherefore, little children are whole, for they are not capable of committing sin; wherefore the curse of Adam is taken from them in me, that it hath no power over them; and the law of circumcision is done away in me.*

And after this manner did the Holy Ghost manifest the word of God unto me; wherefore, my beloved son, I know that it is solemn mockery before God, that ye should baptize little children.

Behold I say unto you that this thing shall ye teach repentance and baptism unto those who are accountable and capable of committing sin; yea, teach parents that they must repent and be baptized, and humble themselves as their little children, and they shall all be saved with their little children.

And their little children need no repentance, neither baptism. Behold, baptism is unto repentance to the fulfilling the commandments unto the remission of sins.

But little children are alive in Christ, even from the foundation of the world; if not so, God is a partial God, and also a changeable God, and a respecter to persons; for how many little children have died without baptism!

Wherefore, if little children could not be saved without baptism, these must have gone to an endless hell.

Behold I say unto you, that he that supposeth that little children need baptism is in the gall of bitterness and in the bonds of iniquity; for he hath neither faith, hope, nor charity; wherefore, should he be cut off while in the thought, he must go down to hell.

For awful is the wickedness to suppose that God saveth one child because of baptism, and the other must perish because he hath no baptism.

Wo be unto them that shall pervert the ways of the Lord after this manner, for they shall perish except they repent. Behold, I speak with boldness, having authority from God; and I fear not what man can do, for perfect love casteth out all fear.

For behold that all little children are alive in Christ, and also all they that are without the law. For the power of redemption cometh on all them that have no law; wherefore, he that is not condemned, or he that is under no condemnation, cannot repent; and unto such baptism availeth nothing—

But it is mockery before God, denying the mercies of Christ, and the power of his Holy Spirit, and putting trust in dead works (Moroni 8:4-16, 22-23).

We believe that parents who have been sealed to their children in the temple, through the power of the Holy Melchizedek Priesthood will be able to be with those children again. The Savior had a special place in His heart for little children, and He taught that if anyone offended one of His little ones, it would be better for them that they had a millstone hanged around their neck, and they had been drowned in the depths of the sea (see Mark 9:42; Luke 17:2). What would be a greater offense than condemning a child to hell, just because he/she died before they had an opportunity to receive the ordinance of baptism? We believe that we will be judged according to the light and knowledge that we possessed here, so both little children who die, and those who are mentally handicapped would be covered by the Atonement of Christ under this definition. I believe that this is truly being saved by grace.

Our concept of "Heaven" and "Hell" also differs quite drastically from that of conventional Christianity. Christ taught that: "In My Father's house are many mansions (John 14:2), and Paul taught the Corinthian saints that there are varying degrees of glory that we will inherit in the resurrection (see 1 Corinthians 15:40-42). We believe that the gift of the resurrection is unconditional, and therefore a gift from the Savior to all who will live on the earth, so this is, in one sense, of being saved by grace. Everyone, regardless of how they lived in this life will be saved from an endless physical separation of their body and their spirit. Nothing we can or will do will impact that gift, it is ours through the grace of the Savior. But our eternal inheritances will vary according to our individual levels of obedience while here in this life.

The Bible usually speaks of hell in terms such as fire and brimstone, whose flame ascendeth up forever. Yet any time the works of Satan are mentioned, it is described as darkness. In fact, those who are guilty of blasphemy against the Holy Ghost are thrust into outer darkness with Satan and his angels. These two descriptions are contradictory in nature. Whenever God is mentioned, it is in conjunction with the terms light and glory. In fact, the Bible says that when Christ comes in His glory, the earth will be burned. It seems to me that the Christian world has the two concepts somewhat flip-flopped. Latter-day Saints don't believe in a hell where the wicked are continually burning, but never consumed. In the book of Mosiah, in the Book of Mormon it reads:

> Therefore if that man repenteth not, and remaineth and dieth an enemy to God, the demands of divine justice do awaken his immortal soul to a lively sense of his own guilt, which doth cause him to shrink from the presence of the Lord, and doth fill his breast with guilt, and pain, and anguish, which is like an unquenchable fire, whose flame ascendeth up forever and ever.
>
> And now I say unto you, that mercy hath no claim on that man; therefore his final doom is to endure a never-ending torment (Mosiah 2:38-39).

It seems that the writers of the scriptures use the imagery of endless fire and brimstone to illustrate the horror of our suffering if we don't choose to take advantage of the Savior's atonement. It is figurative, however, and not literal. Those who warrant this punishment will receive it in the world of spirits as they await their resurrection.

King David received a promise from the Lord that he would not leave his soul in hell (see Psalms 16:10; Acts 2:27-31). If that is the case then there must be an exit from hell as well as an entrance to it. Does all of this sound a bit confusing? Well, that's not surprising, because again, as Peter said, Paul's writings will be misunderstood by much of Christianity. However, from modern revelation the picture becomes much more clear. The scriptures speak of hell as being endless punishment, or eternal punishment. But in the Doctrine and Covenants, a compilation of revelations given by God to Joseph Smith, we read:

> And surely every man must repent or suffer, for I God, am endless.
>
> Nevertheless, it is not written that there shall be no end to this torment, but it is written endless torment. Again, it is written, eternal damnation; wherefore it is more express than other scriptures that it might work upon the hearts of the children of men, altogether for my name's glory.

Wherefore, I will explain unto you the mystery, for it is meet unto you to know even as mine apostles. I speak unto you that are chosen in this thing, even as one that you may enter into my rest.

For, behold, the mystery of godliness, how great is it! For behold, I am endless, and the punishment which is given from my hand is endless punishment, for endless is my name. Wherefore . . . Eternal punishment is God's punishment. Endless punishment is God's punishment (Doctrine and Covenants 19:4, 6-12).

Isn't that an interesting doctrine? It's God's punishment, and since endless and eternal are two of the titles by which He is referred to, His punishments are called by those names. In fact the very name Jehovah, in Hebrew means endless or eternal. It doesn't mean that they are going to go on forever, anymore than hell is a big fire-pit with a red colored Devil wielding a pitchfork. The scriptures speak in symbolism. Those who will ultimately be with Satan forever are going to be in a condition described as outer-darkness (Matthew 25:30). That doesn't sound like a place that contains a whole lot of warmth. In fact it sounds like just the opposite. It sounds dark and cold, and very empty and lonely. It is in this condition of emptiness that those who don't qualify for salvation will spend eternity. So what is hell? The Prophet Nephi again enlightens us on a doctrinal point:

Wherefore, he has given a law; and where there is no law given there is no punishment; and where there is no punishment there is no condemnation; and where there is no condemnation the mercies of the Holy One of Israel have claim upon them, because of the atonement; for they are delivered by the power of him.

For the atonement satisfieth the demands of his justice upon all those who have not the law given to them, that they are delivered from that awful monster, death and hell, and the devil, and the lake of fire and brimstone, which is endless torment (2 Nephi 9:25-26).

In order to be able to abide whatever degree of reward that we inherit, we have to be able to live according to certain laws and principles that will exist there. If we didn't learn obedience, while here in this life, we will apparently get a second chance . . . but with a different teacher. If we haven't repented when our day of reckoning comes we will apparently be turned over to the buffetings (battering or blows) of Satan until the day of redemption.

I guess it's somewhat like being sent to detention in school, or going through rehabilitation for some sort of addiction. We must learn to be a certain type of a person, and if we didn't discipline ourselves here, then we will need to go through hell until we get it right.

For he who is not able to abide the law of a celestial kingdom cannot abide a celestial glory.

And he who cannot abide the law of a terrestrial kingdom cannot abide a terrestrial glory.

And he who cannot abide the law of a telestial kingdom cannot abide a telestial glory; therefore he is not meet for a kingdom of glory. Therefore he must abide a kingdom which is not a kingdom of glory (Doctrine and Covenants 88:22-24).

The other reason that we will be sent to hell is that if we do not repent, we will not have full access to the Savior's Atonement, other than the gift of the resurrection. Christ taught that if we do not repent, we will perish (see Luke 13:3). He also revealed the following to Joseph Smith:

For behold, I, God have suffered these things for all, that they might not suffer if they would repent;

But if would not repent they must suffer even as I;

Which suffering caused myself, even God, the greatest of all, to tremble because of pain, and to bleed at every pore, and to suffer both body and spirit—and would that I might not drink the bitter cup, and shrink—

Nevertheless, glory be to the Father, and I partook and finished my preparations unto the children of men.

Wherefore, I command you again to repent, lest I humble you with my almighty power; and that you confess your sins, lest you suffer these punishments of which I have spoken (Doctrine and Covenants 19:16-20).

There are eternal laws that not even God can fail to observe or he would cease to be God. One of them is that of justice. Paul also speaks of this law on many occasions. It is simply this: every sin that is committed must be atoned for. If we truly repent and change our nature, we will be allowed to have the law of mercy extended to us rather than justice, because Christ will cover us with His Atonement. But if we don't repent we will have to suffer the pain for our own sins. Maybe that is the deeper meaning of the commandment not to take the name of the Lord, our God, in vain. If we profess to be Christians, yet don't repent and take advantage of His Atonement in our behalf, the suffering that He went through for us will for all intents and purposes have been done in vain.

That could also be why He pleads with each of us to: "Come unto me all ye that labor, and are heavy laden, and I will give you rest" (Matthew 11:28). He obviously loved each of us enough to go through with the Atonement, even though He would rather not have had to (see Luke 22:41-42). And knowing what it feels like to suffer as he did, he doesn't want any of us to have to do likewise, especially when He has already paid the price for our ransom. It seems the least we could do would be to repent of the sins we have committed, and try our level best to live our lives the best we possibly can, so we can show to Him our gratitude for His sacrifice in our behalf. After all, He summed it up in one simple phrase: "If ye love me, keep my commandments" (John 14:15).

We are all part of the same eternal family, brothers and sisters, children of the same Eternal Father. Jesus Christ, the only begotten of the Father in the flesh, is our elder brother. He loves all of us the same and though he doesn't play favorites, it is a truth that we can be favored of Him.

The story of the House of Israel is undisputable evidence. We become favored of God by how we live our lives. For every commandment we keep we will receive the blessings, which are associated with that commandment or law. On the other hand, if we fail to adhere to any given commandment we will also inherit the consequences or punishments that are associated with it as well. In that sense, it is not God, but us, that determine the degree to which we are favored of the Father.

We should love all of our Heavenly Father's children, and strive to treat all in the manner that he would treat them. We all have equal access to the Atonement from our birth, but being born into a world of sin, it is possible for us to fall from his grace. When this happens we must show our faith by repentance in order to again lay claim upon the Atonement and its blessings. If we break the word atonement down it is: at/ one/ ment. When we sin we are not "one" with Deity anymore. Faith is an action verb. When we show our faith by humbling ourselves and repenting, we can once again become one with our Heavenly Father and His son Jesus Christ. It is in this condition, that of a broken heart and a contrite spirit, that we will be allowed to return again, to live with them in their presence . . . and Salvation cometh to none else.

No, obedience to the law of Moses, and the ordinances of the lesser priesthood will not save us. But our obedience to the commandments, and the ordinances of the higher priesthood are absolutely essential if we expect to inherit all that our Father has in store for us as His children.

47. For so hath the Lord commanded us, saying, I have set thee
to be a light of the Gentiles, that thou shouldest be for salva-
tion unto the ends of the earth.

—Acts 13:47

CHAPTER 17

WALKING IN THE LIGHT

As the great and dreadful events prophesied of concerning the second coming of the Messiah proceed to unfold before our eyes, the truth regarding religion will be made manifest to the world. Many and great are the events which we will undoubtedly witness. The last days are truly upon us, as evidenced by the unrest and instability which exists in the world today. The Book of Mormon tells us that "it" would be brought forth to be the second witness of Jesus Christ in a day that would be exactly as it is today. Many have claimed that the young man, Joseph Smith, wrote the Book of Mormon as a clever scheme to deceive the world and lead them to follow him and his doctrine, thus bringing glory to him.

Let me quote from one of those so-called made up prophecies, and let you ponder the words yourself. They come from the eighth chapter of Mormon, in the Book of Mormon. They prophesy of the day in which it will come to light to help establish the truth. Ask yourself if they sound like the idle words of an unlearned fourteen-year-old plowboy.

And he that shall breathe out wrath and strife against the work of the Lord, and against the covenant people of the Lord who are the house of Israel, and shall say: We will destroy the work of the Lord, and the Lord will not remember his covenant which he hath made unto the house of Israel—the same is in danger of being hewn down and cast into the fire.

And no one need say that they shall not come, for they surely shall, for the Lord hath spoken it; for out of the earth shall they come, by the hand of the Lord, and none can stay it; and it shall come in a day when it shall be said that miracles are done away and it shall come even as if one should speak from the dead.

And it shall come in a day when the blood of the saints shall cry unto the Lord, because of secret combinations and the works of darkness.

Yea, it shall come in a day that there shall be great pollutions upon the face of the earth; there shall be murders, and robbing, and lying, and deceivings, and whoredoms, and all manner of abominations; when there will be many who will say, do this, or do that, and it mattereth not, for the Lord will uphold such at the last day. But wo unto such, for they are in the gall of bitterness and in the bonds of iniquity.

O ye wicked and perverse and stiff-necked people, why have ye built up churches unto yourselves to get gain? Why have ye transfigured the holy word of God, that ye might bring damnation unto your souls? Behold, look ye unto the revelations of God; for behold, the time cometh at that day when all these things must be fulfilled.

Behold, the Lord hath shown unto me great and marvelous things concerning that, which must shortly come, at that day when these things shall come forth among you.

Behold, I speak unto you as if ye were present, and yet ye are not. But behold, Jesus Christ hath shown you unto me, and I know your doing.

And I know that ye do walk in the pride of your hearts; and there are none save a few only who do not lift themselves up in the pride of their hearts, unto the wearing of very fine apparel, unto envying, and strifes, and malice, and persecutions, and all manner of iniquities; and your churches, yea, even every one, have become polluted because of the pride of your hearts.

For behold, ye do love money, and your substance, and your fine apparel, and the adorning of your churches, more than ye love the poor and the needy, the sick and the afflicted.

O ye pollutions, ye hypocrites, ye teachers who sell yourselves for that which will canker, why have ye polluted the holy church of God? Why are ye ashamed to take upon you the name of Christ? Why do ye not think that greater is the value of an endless happiness than that misery which never dies—because of the praise of the world? (Mormon 8:21, 26-27, 30-31, 33-38).

Now I would ask again, whose words are these? Do they have a familiar ring to them? If they don't, they should. They are not the words of a man, but the words and warnings of a God who is shortly to bring an end to such wickedness as was described by an ancient prophet on this continent, who was allowed to see our day. He foretells of the falling of these churches that he has not ordained to do what they do. In light of these solemn warnings do not be surprised if we witness the corruption and downfall of many prominent denominations and their teachers as the end draws nigh, for it will surely happen.

Bear in mind, and remember that all of this began in the year 1820, less than fifty years after the signers of The Declaration of Independence penned the document that would finally make freedom of religion possible. Before planes and trains and automobiles, and computers, or global satellite systems, I wonder where a veritable teenager who was raised on a small farm in upstate New York in that day and age would have gone to acquire his information for such an undertaking as to write a history of the ancient people of the Americas? Does it really make sense that he would be able to fabricate such a volume on his own? I've always found it interesting that those who fight so hard to try and disprove the work he brought forth to the world so often talk in such a contradictory manner.

So where did he accumulate data that would be verified centuries later, when tools were on the earth that could be used to explore and transmit discoveries? He couldn't get on the Internet and downloaded the information necessary to describe in detail the civilizations, customs, and buildings of ancient South or Central America, or even they Holy Land for that matter. He also couldn't charter a private Lear-Jet and fly down there personally for years to study their cultures and customs, in order to effectively pull off this so-called hoax, and deceive the masses! Where might I ask would a person in America's back-woods in the 1820s, be he educated or not, be able to come up with the kind of research required to write a book of this caliber? A written work, which contains over five hundred pages, and is replete with doctrines and story lines of the Bible? One that is so interwoven with the ancient customs and writing styles of the ancient people of the old world that it has astounded many of the most learned scholars of our modern day?

Many who met the prophet Joseph Smith went away with a new respect for him. Josiah Quincy, former mayor of Boston, after meeting the Prophet Joseph Smith made the following statement about the fact that the world would yet have to account for his claims of being a prophet called of God:

> *"It is by no means improbable that some future textbook, for the use of generations yet unborn, will contain a question something like this: What historical American of the nineteenth century has exerted the most powerful influence upon the destinies of his countrymen? And it is by no means impossible that the answer to that interrogatory may be thus written: Joseph Smith, the Mormon prophet. And the reply, absurd as it doubtless seems to most men now living, may be an obvious commonplace to their descendants. History deals in surprises and paradoxes quite as startling as this. The man who established a religion in this age of free debate, who was and is to-day accepted by hundreds of thousands as a direct emissary from the Most High, such a rare human being is not to be disposed of by pelting his memory with unsavory epithets"* (Josiah Quincy, Figures of the Past, Boston: Little, Brown, and Co.[1883], 376).

Let me quote another statement concerning Joseph Smith:

> *"A Russian historian had visited the United States for something over a year studying the history of great Americans and American institutions. As he was about to board his ship to return to his native land, newspapermen interrogated him. One of them asked him this question: 'In your study of great Americans during this past year, which of them do you consider to be the greatest?' His answer is most startling. He said, 'You have had only one truly great American, one who gave the world ideas that could change the whole destiny of the human race—Joseph Smith, the Mormon Prophet.'"* (William E. Barrett, "The Life and Character of the Prophet Joseph Smith," Speeches of the Year [1964], 2).

111

Count Leo Tolstoi, the great Russian author, statesman, and philosopher, held a similar opinion as to the future destiny of the "American religion" founded under the instrumentality of the Prophet Joseph Smith.

Thomas J. Yates related an experience he had while a student at Cornell University in 1900. He had the privilege of meeting Dr. Andrew W. White, former president of Cornell, and at the time, U. S. ambassador to Germany. Upon learning that Mr. Yates was a Latter-day Saint, Dr. White made an appointment for Mr. Yates to spend an evening with him, at which time he related to him an experience he had with Count Tolstoi while serving as U. S. Foreign Minister to Russia in 1892. Dr. White visited quite often with Count Tolstoi, and upon one occasion they discussed religion. I quote from Elder Yates' account of this discussion as related to him by Dr. White:

'Dr. White,' said Count Tolstoi, I wish you would tell me about your American religion.' 'We have no state church in America,' replied Dr. White. 'I know that, but what about your American religion?'

Patiently the Dr. White explained to the Count that in America there are many religions, and that each person is free to belong to the particular church in which he is interested.

To this Tolstoi impatiently replied: ' I know all of this, but I want to know about the American religion. Catholicism originated in Rome; the Episcopal Church originated in England; the Lutheran Church in Germany, but the Church to which I refer originated in America, and is commonly known as the Mormon Church. What can you tell me of the teachings of the Mormon Church? What can you tell me of the the teachings of the Mormons?'

'Well', said Dr. White, 'I know very little concerning them. They have an unsavory reputation, they practice polygamy, and are very superstitious.'

The Count Leo Tolstoi, in his honest and stern, but lovable manner, rebuked the ambassador. 'Dr. White, I am greatly surprised and disappointed that a man of your great learning and position should be so ignorant on this important subject. The Mormon people teach the American religion; their principles teach the people not only of Heaven and its attendant glories, but how to live so that their social and economic relations with each other are placed on a sound basis. If the people follow the teachings of this Church, nothing can stop their progress—it will be limitless. There have been great *movements started in the past but they have died or been modified before they reached maturity. If Mormonism is able to endure, unmodified, until it reaches the third and fourth generations, it is destined to become the greatest power the world has ever known"* (LeGrand Richards, A Marvelous Work and a Wonder, 435-36).

These are impressive summations on the part of men who were not affiliated with the church Joseph Smith restored to the earth. The true greatness of this modern Prophet is found not only in the fact that he gave the world ideas that could change its destiny, but in the fact that he lived those God-given principles and integrated them into his person. Those inspired principles were an integral part of who he was—even a prophet of God. The testimony of Count Leo Tolstoi verifies what the Prophet Daniel said of the Savior's church in the last days. He said it would be as a stone cut out of the mountain without hands, that would roll forth consuming all other kingdoms in its path (see Daniel 2:44-45). If this truly is that Church, nothing can stand in its way or halt its progress. It will fill the whole earth in preparation for the day the scriptures speak of, that the Bride will present herself unto the Bridegroom (see Revelation 21:2), in preparation for the thousand years of peace in which the Messiah will reign personally upon the earth, after He destroys all wickedness from off its face.

To further lend credence to the Latter-day Saints position in regard to the importance of the veracity of both Joseph Smith and the Book of Mormon, I quote a latter-day apostle's words on the matter:

Either the Book of Mormon is what the prophet Joseph said it is or this church and its founder are false . . .fraudulent . . . a deception from the first instance. Now not everything in life is so black and white, but it seems that the authenticity of the Book of Mormon, and its keystone role in our belief is exactly that. Either Joseph Smith was the prophet he said he was, who after seeing the Father and the Son, later beheld the Angel Moroni . . . repeatedly heard counsel from his lips, eventually receiving at his hand a set of ancient gold plates, which he then translated according to the gift and power of God . . . or else he did not. And if he did not, he is not entitled to retain even the reputation of New England folk hero . . . or well meaning young man . . . or writer of remarkable fiction . . . No, and he's not entitled to be considered a great teacher, or a quintessential American prophet . . . if he lied about the coming forth of the Book of Mormon, he's certainly none of those" (Elder Jeffrey R. Holland; CES Symposium, Aug. 1994).

It is my witness that Joseph Smith was indeed the prophet of the Restoration that the Savior raised up in these last days, and through whom he would restore light and truth and priesthood authority to the earth. When Joseph and his wife Emma rode to the Hill Cumorah on that eventful morning to receive the sacred plates of gold, they did so in a buckboard, drawn by a horse. Have you ever considered why man was still using the same mode of travel that Pharaoh used to chase down Moses and the fleeing Israelites thousands of years earlier?

Since the time the priesthood of God was restored to the earth and the ancient record of Joseph was finally brought to light, light has flooded the earth. Why so little technology on the earth for thousands of years, and then in the past two centuries we've gone from horse and buggy, to the moon? That, two centuries ago in order to communicate, we needed to travel to do so, or send by pony express our correspondence, and now all we need to do is plug in our modems, or tune in our satellites? Maybe we're just so much more intelligent than all who came before us. Or could it be that the explosion of knowledge and technology has come because light has once again been restored to the earth? Maybe it's just a coincidence, but then again maybe it's not. Let's talk about light as it is spoken of in the scriptures. As I mentioned in the previous chapter, whenever darkness is mentioned, it is associated with Satan and his works. Light, is used by the prophets to describe the things of God. Have you ever wondered why that is the case?

Picture a darkened room at midday. If we were to open the blinds, the room would immediately be flooded with light, which would displace the darkness. Now let's reverse the situation for a minute. Imagine being in a lighted room at midnight. If we open the blinds will the room suddenly be flooded with the darkness from outside? Of course not. But . . . why? What is there about light that makes it so different from darkness? Light will repel darkness, but darkness has no power over light. In fact, all that darkness appears to be is the absence of light. It is when we walk in the light that we are not afraid. As an example of this, when is the best time to watch a scary movie? When it's light we can see what's there, but in darkness we are unsure. In the same manner, Satan does his best work in darkness. If he can get each of us to so live that we aren't in tune with the Holy Ghost, then the light will flee from us and we will walk in darkness as noonday (Isaiah 59:9-10; Doctrine and Covenants 95:5-6).

The modern-day technology that we so enjoy isn't just for our enjoyment. It has come forth to allow Ephraim to finally gather God's children, from the four corners of the earth. Today, as never before, the Lord has given to man the capability to spread the gospel cause to all the earth. James offers to us the key to walking within that light. "Submit yourselves therefore to God. Resist the devil, and he will flee from you. Draw nigh unto God, and he will draw nigh unto you" (James 4:7-8). Our Father in Heaven would have all of his children to walk in the light. We must each choose for ourselves if we will do so.

A glorious day is upon us. The light of the truth is available to all who will abide it . . . but will we? There are many today who love darkness more than light. They are blinded by traditions and teachings of men: "And that wicked one cometh and taketh away light and truth through disobedience, from the children of men, because of the traditions of their fathers (Doctrine and Covenants 93:39). May we all seek for the light and not turn it away when it is offered to us.

As I close this chapter, I do so with the words of that very angel who delivered the sacred record to Joseph Smith:

And I exhort you to remember these things; for the time speedily cometh that ye shall know that I lie not, for ye shall see me at the bar of God; and the Lord God will say unto you: Did I not declare my words unto you, which were written by this man, like as one crying from the dead, yea, even as one speaking out of the dust? And God shall show unto you, that that which I have written is true. (Moroni 10:27, 29)

It is evident from his words that the burden of proof has been transferred from his shoulders, and placed squarely upon ours. If we have access to his words while in this life, but fail to give heed to them, along with those of the rest of the prophets whose words fill the sacred record of the stick of Joseph, we will someday stand before our Savior without excuse.

It is my desire that the information in this book will in some way inspire those who read it to accept the invitation from the birthright tribe of Ephraim to seek the light that the gospel offers. Our Heavenly Father has revealed, and continues to reveal through a living prophet, the truths which we will need to survive the trials, which lie ahead. It is only when we walk in darkness that we shall fear the future (Doctrine and Covenants 38:30). May He bless us all, in our continuing quest for truth, that we may stand as witnesses of Him at all times and in all things.

CHAPTER 18
EPILOGUE

Joseph Smith was once asked what we, as members of the Church of Jesus Christ of Latter-day Saints believe. He responded by drafting thirteen items, which he termed as the "Articles of Faith." They are as follows:

1. We believe in God, the Eternal Father, and in His Son, Jesus Christ, and in the Holy Ghost.
2. We believe that men will be punished for their sins, and not for Adam's transgression.
3. We believe that through the Atonement of Christ, all mankind may be saved, by obedience to the laws and ordinances of the gospel.
4. We believe that the first principles and ordinances of the Gospel are: first, Faith in the Lord Jesus Christ; second, Repentance; third, Baptism by immersion for the remission of sins; fourth, Laying on of hands for the gift of the Holy Ghost.
5. We believe that a man must be called of God, by prophecy, and by the laying on of hands by those who are in authority, to preach the gospel and administer in the ordinances thereof.
6. We believe in the same organization that existed in the Primitive Church, namely, apostles, prophets, pastors, teachers, evangelists, and so forth.
7. We believe in the gift of tongues, prophecy, revelation, visions, healing, interpretation of tongues, and so forth.
8. We believe the Bible to be the word of God as far as it is translated correctly; we also believe the Book of Mormon to be the word of God.
9. We believe all that God has revealed, all that He does

now reveal, and we believe that He will yet reveal many great and important things pertaining to the Kingdom of God.

10. We believe in the literal gathering of Israel and in the restoration of the Ten Tribes; that Zion (the New Jerusalem) will be built upon the American continent; that Christ will reign personally upon the earth; and, that the earth will be renewed and receive its paradisiacal glory.

11. We claim the privilege of worshipping Almighty God according to the dictates of our own conscience, and allow all men the same privilege, let them worship how, where, or what they may.

12. We believe in being subject to kings, presidents, rulers, and magistrates, in obeying, honoring, and sustaining the law.

13. We believe in being honest, true, chaste, benevolent, virtuous, and in doing good to all men; indeed, we may say we follow the admonition of Paul—We believe all things, we hope all things, we have endured many things, and hope to be able to endure all things. If there is anything virtuous, lovely, or of good report, or praiseworthy, we seek after these things. (*History of the Church, Vol. 4, 535-541*).

These thirteen articles encompass virtually all the things that the Savior has asked each of us to strive for in this life. He also told us something very important to look for when searching for his true people:

> *Beware of false prophets, which come to you in sheep's clothing, but inwardly they are ravening wolves.*

> *Ye shall know them by their fruits. Do men gather grapes of thorns, or figs of thistles?*

> *Even so every good tree bringeth forth good fruit; but a corrupt tree bringeth forth evil fruit.*

A good tree cannot bring forth evil fruit, neither can a corrupt tree bring forth good fruit.

Every tree that bringeth not forth good fruit is hewn down, and cast into the fire.

Wherefore by their fruits ye shall know them (Matthew 7:15-20).

There you have it, evil cannot bring forth good.

I was recently invited to address a congregation of baseball players at a Sunday morning chapel service, at one of the major league baseball parks, by a friend who is a very good man, and devout Southern Baptist. As I traveled to the east to do so, I was given the news by him that he had just been informed by the powers that be, that I would not be allowed to speak after all. He then apologized, and said that he wasn't aware that things worked that way back there, but when he told them that I was a "Mormon," they said that only "Christians" could speak at their services, and that Mormons aren't Christians, so the offer had been withdrawn.

This good man knows me, and knows what I represent as a religious educator in the Church's Educational System. He was a bit miffed by their reaction. I held no ill feelings for the people who rejected my services, and especially none toward him. I have encountered many people who through ignorance or misinformation have treated the church and me similarly. I rendered two years of my young life at the age of 19 to trying to spread the good news of the gospel. I did so as every other young man or woman does, without pay, and at the expense of my own family. Many people thought that I was more than just a little bit crazy to have left my home at such a critical time in my life to do what I was doing. When asked why I did it, my reply is quite simple: our message is true, and I am a member of the tribe of Ephraim. If we didn't go and tell the world of the gospel truths, and offer them the ordinances of salvation, they would probably never receive them in this life. Now how could I ever attach a price tag on that? Where much is given, much is required, and I have been privileged to have had the truth from my earliest understanding. I have grown up knowing what most seekers of truth would give anything to know. So it is my responsibility, and my privilege, to share these blessings with all I can find, which seek them.

The Savior set up the Church before he left with the emphasis upon missionary work. In fact that is what Peter, Paul, and the rest of the Lord's chosen apostles spent their entire lifetimes doing. He sent missionaries out two-by-two to preach the gospel, to bring as many people into the fold of the Good Shepherd as possible. Before departing he gave his disciples this command, which is a sign of the true and living church: "And when thou art converted, strengthen thy brethren" (see Luke 22:32). The Lord revealed this to the prophet Joseph Smith concerning the duty and responsibility of Ephraim in the last days: "Behold, I sent you out to testify and warn the people, and it becometh every man who hath been warned to warn his neighbor" (Doctrine and Covenants 88:81).

A prophet of God, President Gordon B. Hinckley, has said that we are not trying to take anybody's truth from them, but rather we ask that they bring the truth that they now have, and let us see if we can add to it. Anyone who has known this great man knows of his fruits. He is a man of character and goodness, and there is not an evil bone in his body. He is a man of God, and more . . . he is a Prophet of God, just as every prophet before him, modern or ancient. Just as Moses led the children of Egypt safely through their wilderness, and the Red Sea on dry ground, so he has been given to us to lead us through our modern wilderness. Never has evil been so united together to destroy the souls of men, as it is today. There has never been a time when our Father's children have needed the guidance of a living prophet as today. As one browses the Articles of Faith, and as the world had occasion to visit Salt Lake City for the 2002 Olympic Games and see first hand, I would challenge anyone to show with any real validity, evil fruits from the Church of Jesus Christ of Latter-day Saints. Its teachings are as Christian as any church on the earth, and I would dare say more so.

Those who fight against the church by false allegations, do so in vain, for as Gamaliel told the Pharisees who were persecuting Peter and the apostles after Christ's death and resurrection:

> *Ye men of Israel, take heed to yourselves to yourselves what ye intend to do as touching these men.*
>
> *For before these days rose up Theudas, boasting himself to be somebody; to whom a number of men, about four hundred, joined themselves: who was slain; and all, as many as obeyed him, were scattered, and brought to nought.*
>
> *After this man rose up Judas of Galilee in the days of the taxing, and drew away much people after him: he also perished: and all, even as many as obeyed him, were dispersed.*
>
> *And now I say unto you, refrain from these men, and let them alone: for if this counsel or this work be of men, it will come to nought:*
>
> *But if it be of God, ye cannot overthrow it; lest haply ye be found even to fight against God (Acts 5:35-39).*

As in days of old, we offer that selfsame counsel to the world today.

The evil men who stormed Carthage Jail on that dark June 27th, 1844, and martyred Joseph Smith, the prophet of the restoration, thought that with his death, would come the end of "His Church." However, what they hadn't figured into their equation was that it wasn't Joseph Smith's church. In reality, it was the Savior's church. That same church is still on the earth today, and as the storm of venom and opposition has raged on, so has its numbers increased. This is the work of God, and no man can stop its progress. Like it or not, the gospel will go forth to every nation, kindred tongue, and people, by the feet of humble missionaries, who like the ones of old, are willing to lay all on the altar to heed the Master's call.

It is my invitation to all who have occasion to read this, to put Moroni's promise to the test. Prayerfully read the Book of Mormon, and ask yourself the question at the end of each page, could any man have written this book? Let alone an obscure 14-year-old farm boy, with very little formal education.

Ephraim's calling in the last days is to gather the elect from the four corners of the earth. In regard to that responsibility, the Savior revealed this to that young farm boy: "And ye are called to bring to pass the gathering of mine elect; for mine elect hear my voice and harden not their hearts" (Doctrine and Covenants 29:7).

If you are the elect of God, the honest of heart, you will know the answer to that question by the power of the Holy Ghost, and in the words of the apostle John "You shall know the truth, and the truth shall set you free."

LIST OF SOURCES

King James Bible: Old Testament/New Testament

LDS Bible Dictionary

The Book of Mormon

The Doctrine and Covenants

The Pearl of Great Price

Religion 302 Institute St. Manual

Old Testament: Holy Land and Jewish Insights
  By Daniel Rona

The Teachings of Spencer W. Kimball
  By Edward Kimball

Jeffrey R. Holland
  CES Symposium Address, August 1994

Dallin H. Oaks
  BYU Fireside Address August 1990

Believing Christ/Following Christ
  By Stephen Robinson

A Marvelous Work And A Wonder
  By LeGrand Richards

THE PLAN OF SALVATION

PRE-MORTAL EXISTENCE
We lived with our Heavenly Father as His spirit children
(Jeremiah 1:5, Abraham 3:22-23)

EARTH-LIFE/BIRTH
Purposes of Mortal Life:
1. To obtain a physical body (1 Cor. 3:16-17)
2. Develop faith: be tested to see if we would keep his commandments when not in his presence (1 Thes 3:7-10)
3. Receive the ordinances of salvation (John 3:5, Isaiah 24:5, 1 Cor. 11:1-2)
4. Provide physical bodies for other spirits (Gen. 1:27-28)
5. Obtain knowledge/ Experiences (Luke 5:2, Hebrews 5:8-9)
6. Death/Spirit World
Two Conditions: Paradise/Spirit Prison (hell)
(2 Cor. 12:4, 1 Peter 3:19)

RESURRECTION
Christ's gift to all born on Earth (Acts 24:15, Alma 11:44-45)

THE JUDGMENT
(1 Sam. 2:10, John 5:20-22)

ASSIGNMENT TO WHATEVER ETERNAL REWARD WE MERITED
(1 Cor. 15:40-42, Alma 11:40-43, 2 Nephi 9:15-16, Doctrine and Covenants 76)

COVENANT LINEAGE

ABRAHAM

<table>
<tr><td>Hagar</td><td>Sarah</td></tr>
<tr><td>Ishmael</td><td>**Isaac (Rebekah)</td></tr>
<tr><td>(Father of Arab nations)</td><td>**Jacob (Israel)/ Esau</td></tr>
</table>

TRIBES OF ISRAEL

Leah	Zilpah	Rachel	Bilhah
Reuben*	Gad*	**Joseph	Dan*
Simeon*	Asher*	Benjamin	Naphtali*
Levi			
Judah			
Issachar*			
Zebulun*			

Adopted into Israel as Tribes

**Ephraim*

Manasseh*

A remnant of Ephraim was to be raised up in the latter-days to gather and preside over scattered Israel.

Lehi was of the tribe of Joseph through Manasseh.

Joseph Smith was a descendant of Ephraim and also the lineage of Judah. He was raised up to be the prophet of the Restoration.

Denotes Lost Tribe
**Denotes Birthright Son*

SCRIPTURAL DATA

God establishes His covenant with Abraham: Gen. 12:2-3; 17:4-8; 22:15-18

The covenant to continue through Isaac: Gen. 21:1-12

Jacob to inherit birthright, have dominion, and preside in family and over nations: Gen. 25:21-23, 29-34; 26:1-5; 27:1-29, 41

Jacob's name changed to Israel: Gen. 32:24-28

Israel designated to be God's chosen people: Deut. 32:7-9

The beginning of the tribes of Israel: Gen. 35:23-26

Blessings of the tribes of Israel: Gen. 49:1-27

Joseph is given birthright: 1 Chr. 5:1-2

Ephraim and Manasseh are adopted as equal tribes: Gen. 48:5-22

Scattered Israel to be gathered by Ephraim in the last days: Jer. 31:6-11

Joseph's seed to gather Israel: 2 Ne. 3:3-4

Judah will be brought to a knowledge of Jesus Christ as their Messiah: Gen. 49:9, D&C 45:51-53

Joseph's seed will take the gospel to all the earth: Deut. 33:16-17, D&C 133:26-34; 64:35-36

Records to be kept for both Judah and Joseph: They must be used together as one in the last days to establish true doctrines: Ezek. 37:15-22; 2 Ne. 3:12

Israel will be preserved/gathered: Amos 9

God will be gracious to the remnant of Joseph: Amos 5:15

Others of the House of Israel existed and must be taught: John 10:16; 3 Ne. 15:20-21

The prophet Lehi was of the House of Joseph: 1 Ne. 5:10-19; Alma 10:3

God shows Lehi of the destruction of Jerusalem: 1 Ne. 1:4-13

Lehi is commanded to leave Jerusalem, the covenant with Abraham and Jacob is honored, and Joseph's seed is preserved: 1 Ne. 2:1-5

Jerusalem was destroyed just as was prophesied: Jer. 52:2; Kings 24-25

Prophecy that the gospel would be taken from the Earth: Amos 8:11-12

An apostasy must occur before the Savior's Second Coming: 2 Thes. 3:19-20

The gospel must be restored in its fulness to the Earth before the Second Coming: Acts 3:19-20

An angel (Moroni) would be sent to help restore that gospel to the Earth: Rev. 14:6-7

Prophecy of the coming forth of the Book of Mormon: Isa. 29:9-14, 18

Israel to be gathered in the last days: Isa. 11:10-13

Ephraim must gather scattered Israel—He is the only one with the authority to do so, being the birthright son: Ezek. 37:19-22; Jer. 31:6-14; Deut. 33:13-17

The Prophet Joseph Smith was a literal descendant of Joseph through Ephraim, which authorized him to begin the Latter-day gathering of Israel: 2 Ne. 3:1-18; D&C 113:3-6; 132:30

We will all be able to know the truthfulness of all things by the power of the Holy Ghost: Eph. 1:17-18; 1 Thes. 1:5; Moro. 10:3-5

ABRAHAM'S SEED AND COVENANT

SPECIAL DESIGNATION OF A CHOSEN LINEAGE
Covenant established: Abraham/Isaac/Jacob (Israel)

Genesis 17:1; 18:1-14; 27:46; 28:1-10; 28:11-22

Exodus 2:23-25; 3:5-10, 15-23; 5:1; 6:5-8; 9:1; 10:3-11; 13:11, 19; 16:1-4

Leviticus 26:41-46

1 Chronicles 16:7-29

Psalms 105; 106:1-8, 21-48

THE BIRTHRIGHT
Genesis 25:29-34; 27:1-41; 43:33; 46:20; 48:1-20

1 Chronicles 5:1-3

Deuteronomy 33:1-17, 28-29; 33:17

Joshua 14:1-4; 17:17

Judges 8:2

Psalms 60:7; 108:8

Isaiah 11

Jeremiah 7:1-16; 31:1-20

Ezekiel 37

Zechariah 9:12; 10:12

Hosea 4-14; 10:11

THE GATHERING OF ISRAEL
Deuteronomy 4:29; 30:3

Psalms 107:3; 147:2

Isaiah 5:26; 6:13; 10:22; 11:11; 27:12; 35:10; 43:5; 49:18; 51:11; 54:7; 56:8

Jeremiah 29:14; 32:37; 23:3; 3:17; 12:15; 16:14-21; 30:3; 31:10; 50:4,19

Nehemiah 1:19

THE GATHERING OF ISRAEL (CONTINUED)

Joel 2:32

Ezekiel 11:17; 20:41; 22:19; 28:25; 34:12 (ALL); 36:24; 37:12; 37:21-28; 39:27

Hosea 1:11

Amos 9:14 (ALL)

Micah 2:12; 4:6

Zechariah 10:8

Matthew 23:37

Luke 13:34

John 11:52

Ephesians 1:10

Doctrine and Covenants 133:25-35

ABRAHAM
ISAAC
JACOB (ISRAEL)

NORTHERN KINGDOM (ISRAEL)	SOUTHERN KINGDOM (JUDAH)

REUBEN	**JUDAH**
SIMEON	**BENJAMIN**
LEVI (Aaronic Priesthood)	
ZEBULUN	TAKEN CAPTIVE
ISSACHAR	INTO BABYLON
DAN	*(Jeremiah 52)*
GAD	*(587 BC)*
ASHER	
NAPHTALI	COMMENCEMENT OF
JOSEPH	PERSIAN EMPIRE
	(559 BC)
	COMMISSION TO
MANASSEH	REBUILD JERUSALEM
EPHRAIM	*(Cyrus 537 BC)*
	PERSIA CONQUERED
	BY EGYPT
	(330 BC)
TAKEN CAPTIVE AND	
SCATTERED . . . LOST	EGYPT BECOMES
(721 BC) (2 Kings 17)	A ROMAN PROVINCE
	(30 BC)
REMNANT SPARED	
(1 Nephi 6:2)	

ABOUT THE AUTHOR

Douglas T. Bentley was born and raised in St. George, Utah, the fourth of six children. He was an accomplished athlete during his formative years, and graduated from Dixie High School in 1975, having played on five different State Championship athletic teams. He was a three- sport letterman, earning letters in football, baseball, and basketball, and received All-State and All-America accolades in football, and All-State status in baseball.

He served two years as a full-time missionary for the Church of Jesus Christ of Latter-day Saints, spending time in Washington and Oregon, while being assigned to both the Seattle and Spokane, Washington Missions. It was during this service that he discovered his passion for sharing the Gospel of Jesus Christ. He found it to be so rewarding to see the joy that the gospel brought into peoples lives that he decided to devote the rest of his life teaching it. His first love had always been sports, but he gave up those pursuits to try and do something that would "Really make a difference in people's lives."

He attended Dixie Junior College and graduated from there

with an Associates Degree in 1979. He then attended Southern Utah State College, in Cedar City, Utah, graduating in 1981 with a Bachelor of Arts Degree in psychology. He graduated from Idaho State University in 1986 with a Masters Degree in Athletic Administration, and received a Master of the Scriptures through CES after finishing a four-year course of study in the Standard Works.

Upon receiving his Bachelors Degree in 1981, he was employed by the Church of Jesus Christ of Latter-day Saints as a religion teacher. He is currently in his third decade of teaching the gospel in the Church Educational System. He has been a licensed financial services agent, and in his spare time he enjoys writing country music. He enjoys hunting and fishing, and being in the outdoors, and has guided several groups on fishing trips to Alaska. Brother Bentley has long been a requested youth speaker. His sense of humor and down- to earth teaching style have made him a popular speaker at youth firesides as well as at Especially For Youth for many years.

He and his wife Deonn have four children, and one grandson. Their oldest son Brock served a two-year mission in The Brazil-Marilia, and Florida-Tampa Missions, and their second son Travis served a mission in the Oklahoma-Tulsa Mission. Their youngest two children, Logan and Brianne are presently living with them at home in St. George.

0   26575 77069   8